STEP-BY-STEP

TABLE
DECORATING

*This book is dedicated to
my mother, Xamie, and my late father,
Morris Levitte.*

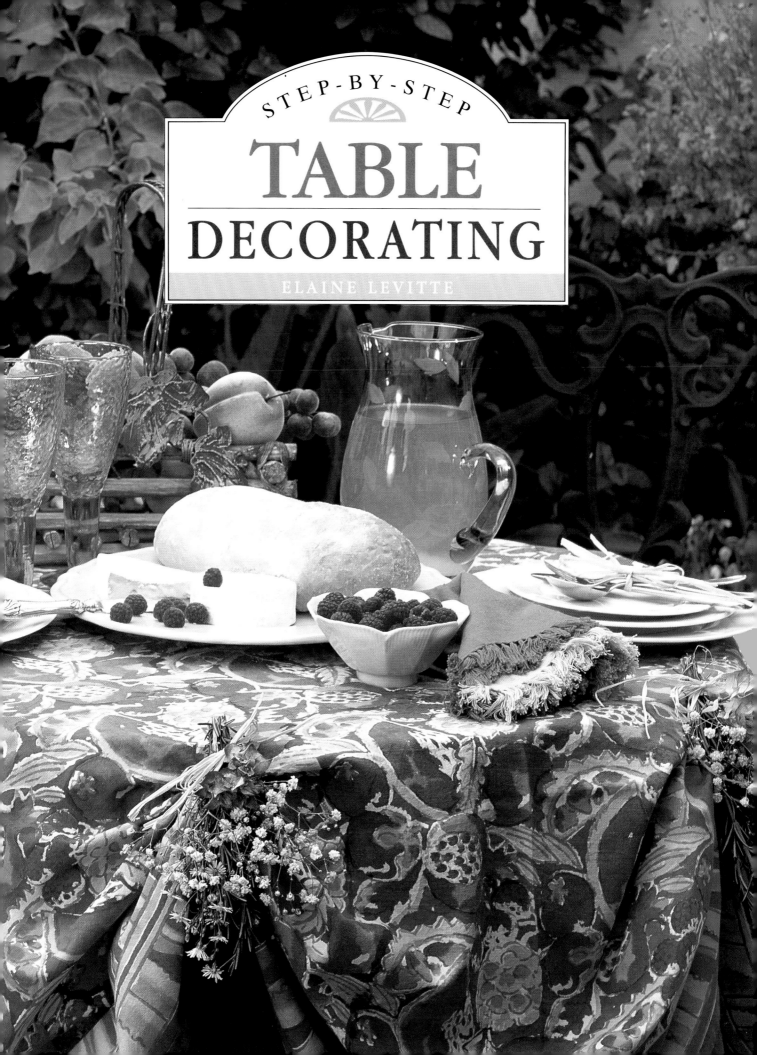

STEP-BY-STEP

TABLE
DECORATING

ELAINE LEVITTE

Contents

INTRODUCTION

The decorated table

The success of a meal relies on more than just good food. A beautifully laid table goes a long way to creating the right ambience for a truly memorable meal. And there is no need to spend a fortune on the finest linen, crockery and cutlery. Of course these objects are great decorating aids, but this book is dedicated to those of you who enjoy the challenge of doing it yourself. In the following chapters you will learn how easy it is to create a range of exciting settings with hand-crafted objects, and without any special skills.

There are very few rules when it comes to table decorating, and many of these can be broken. Those that can't are adhered to mainly for practical reasons. For example, a centrepiece should be either low enough to see over or elevated on a support that will not obstruct the view across the table.

Another consideration is lighting. As romantic as dinner by candlelight may sound, it is still important to be able to see what you are eating and drinking, so make sure that you either use enough candles or supplement the candlelight with another light source. On the other hand, bright, direct light may be appropriate for a regular family dinner, but it is unlikely to do anything for that special atmosphere you would like to create when entertaining.

Although some celebrations still call for formal table settings, these tend to be the exception rather than the rule. The current trend favours a far more casual approach to dining, and correspondingly informal settings reflect this trend. Who dictates that knives, forks and spoons must be laid out like soldiers on either side of a dinner plate? And does it really matter if the side plate is placed above the dinner plate rather than on its left? Be bold and lend a lighthearted approach to your table settings. Try tying the cutlery in a bundle with a beautiful piece of ribbon and placing it on the dinner plate. Or go for the eclectic look with an interesting selection of mismatched crockery, cutlery and glassware. If you prefer to play it safe, stick to basic white plates that can be dressed up or down to suit the occasion. An all-white table setting with crisply starched cloth and napkins will always look elegant, but if you prefer, you could ring the changes by introducing brightly coloured or patterned accessories such as a hand-painted cloth, checked napkins or a vase of gay spring flowers.

But don't wait for a special occasion before putting some basic table-decorating ideas into practice. A little bit of effort can turn an ordinary meal into a memorable one — then just wait for the compliments to roll in!

CHAPTER ONE

Bright for breakfast

Start the day on a bright note at a table set with a colourful
assortment of crockery and glassware on a special hand-stencilled cloth.
Coordinating napkins together with a croissant tray and an
informal floral arrangement complete the picture.

The basic cloth

Making a plain tablecloth is simplicity itself, no matter what the shape or size of your table.
The cloth can be decorated in a variety of ways to suit your tastes and needs.

M A T E R I A L S & E Q U I P M E N T

♦ Cotton fabric (quantity will depend on the
size of the table – see STEP 1)
♦ Sewing thread to match the fabric
♦ Tape measure
♦ Scissors
FOR A ROUND CLOTH YOU WILL ALSO NEED:
♦ A drawing pin
♦ A length of string
♦ A pencil
♦ Brown paper or newsprint (optional)

R O U N D   C L O T H

1. *Measure the diameter of the tabletop. Add 60 cm (24 in) to this measurement – this allows for a 5 cm (2 in) hem all round and a 25 cm (10 in) drop.*

2. *Cut out a square of fabric with sides as long as the total diameter calculated above. If the fabric is not wide enough, joins will be necessary. Instead of one seam down the centre, join an extra strip of fabric to either side of a central panel, keeping the side panels equal widths (DIAGRAM 1).*

3. *Fold the fabric in quarters. Work on a flat surface into which you can insert a drawing pin, and do so at the corner of the folded square which is the centre of the piece of fabric (DIAGRAM 2). Tie a length of string to the pin and attach a pencil to the other end of the string so that the point of the pencil is on the opposite edge of the folded square. Holding the pencil upright, draw a quarter circle on the fabric by carefully moving the pencil across from corner to corner (DIAGRAM 2). Cut along the line through all four layers of fabric. If you prefer, you can use this method to make a paper pattern before cutting the fabric.*

4. *Machine- or hand-stitch a 5 cm (2 in) hem all round.*

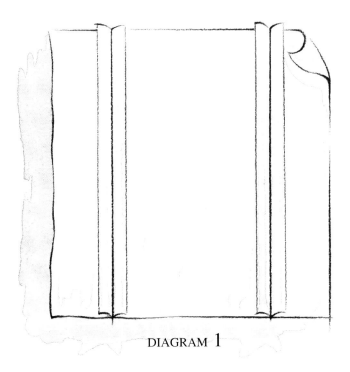

DIAGRAM **1**

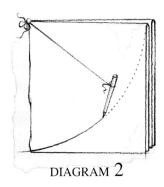

DIAGRAM **2**

S Q U A R E   O R   R E C T A N G U L A R   C L O T H

1. *Measure the length and width of the top of the table and add 60 cm (24 in) to each measurement. This includes 5 cm (2 in) for the hems, and will give the cloth a 25 cm (10 in) drop all round.*

2. *Cut out the required shape to the calculated size, along the grain of the fabric. Turn in the edges twice by 2.5 cm (1 in) to form a neat hem. Stitch the hem down along all four edges.*

The painted cloth

Fabric painting is simple and fun. Draw inspiration from a favourite plate or mug with a clearly defined design that is easy to duplicate. You may feel confident enough to paint your fabric freehand, but easy-to-cut stencils will ensure uniformity of design while maintaining a hand-crafted look.

MATERIALS & EQUIPMENT

- ◆ Plain cloth made up as described on PAGE 11
- ◆ Fabric paints in the colours of your choice
- ◆ Tracing paper
- ◆ Pencil
- ◆ Stencil card or clear acetate film
- ◆ Fine-tipped permanent marker (if using acetate film)
- ◆ Sharp craft knife
- ◆ Masking tape
- ◆ Sponge
- ◆ Paper towel or newspaper
- ◆ Iron

1. *Draw or trace your chosen design and use a photocopier to enlarge it to the desired size. If the design source, for example a plate, can be placed straight onto a photocopier, this will make the job much easier.*

2. *A separate stencil is required for each colour of the design. Clear acetate film will allow you to trace directly off your artwork with a permanent marker. If you are using opaque stencil card, trace the outline of each colour off the artwork separately and transfer it onto the stencil card. Make sure that each piece of card or acetate is at least 10 cm (4 in) bigger than your design in width and length.*

3. *Using a craft knife, carefully cut out the stencils for each colour from the sheets of acetate or card (PHOTO 1).*

4. *Position the first stencil on the cloth and secure it with masking tape. Cut a piece of sponge that is easy to grip with your fingertips.*

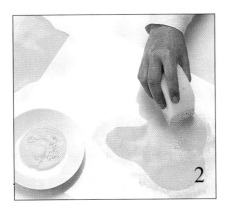

5. *Dip the sponge in the paint and dab off any excess paint on a piece of paper towel or newspaper – very little paint is required and the sponge should be as dry as possible to prevent 'bleeding' under the edges of the stencil. Apply the paint to the cut-out area of the stencil with a dabbing motion* (PHOTO 2). *Don't worry if the paint looks blotchy when wet – it is a very forgiving medium and*

dries to a subtle finish. In any case, irregularities in colour intensity create interesting results.

6. *Carefully remove the stencil and reposition it to repeat the design. As you will need to use very little paint, it will dry very quickly and you can proceed with your next colour almost straight away. To do this, superimpose your*

second stencil over the dry painted area and sponge on the second colour with another sponge (PHOTO 3). *Repeat this process until all colours are applied.*

7. *To fix the paint, iron on the reverse side of the cloth at the maximum temperature suggested for the material, going over each stencilled area for about three minutes* (PHOTO 4).

The napkins

For a 30 cm (12 in) square napkin, cut a piece of fabric 35 cm (14 in) square. Stitch in a 2.5 cm (1 in) hem around all four sides, then stencil them so that they match the tablecloth. Scale down the design and recut smaller stencils, or use the same ones that you used to print the tablecloth. Although the stencil design used to print the tablecloth may well be out of proportion to the size of the napkin, an interesting effect can be achieved by positioning these larger stencils so that parts of the design run off the edge of the napkin. If you like, you could also stitch each printed napkin to a larger piece of hemmed fabric to give it a border – using the same material that you use to make the croissant tray will create a well-coordinated effect.

The croissant tray

Mix and match your fabrics and ribbons to make this attractive, reversible tray
for serving croissants, scones or rolls at the table.

MATERIALS & EQUIPMENT

- ◆ 0.5 m (½ yd) each of two contrasting colours of cotton fabric
- ◆ 1.3 m (1½ yds) ribbon about 9 mm (⅜ in) wide; colour to match or contrast with your fabric
- ◆ Sewing thread to match the ribbons
- ◆ An A3 sheet of stiff cardboard
- ◆ Tape measure
- ◆ Scissors
- ◆ Ruler
- ◆ Dressmakers' pencil
- ◆ Pins
- ◆ Sewing machine

1. *Cut a square 38 cm x 38 cm (15 in x 15 in) from each fabric. Pin the two squares together with right sides facing.*

2. *Draw a stitching line 7 cm (2¾ in) in from each edge of the material using a dressmakers' pencil (DIAGRAM 1).*

3. *Cut the ribbon into eight 16 cm (6¼ in) lengths. Pin these between the two pieces of fabric at the stitching lines,*

4 cm (⅝ in) from the edges of the fabric, securing 1 cm (⅜ in) of each ribbon into the stitching line. The remaining 15 cm (6 in) of ribbon must lie to the inside of the stitching line (DIAGRAM 2).

4. *Using the dotted lines in DIAGRAM 3 as a guide, stitch around the fabric, 1 cm (⅜ in) in from the long edges and 7 cm (2¾ in) in at the corners, leaving one edge open.*

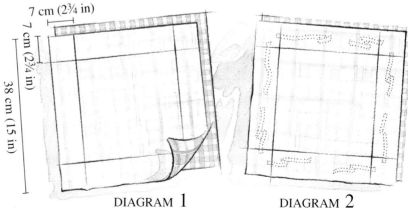

7 cm (2¾ in)

7 cm (2¾ in)

38 cm (15 in)

DIAGRAM 1

DIAGRAM 2

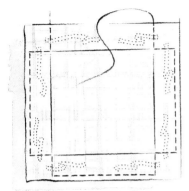

DIAGRAM 3

5. *Trim away excess fabric close to the stitching line before turning right side out. Press the seams flat. The ribbons should now be anchored into the seams at the centre of each short side.*

6. *Cut one piece of cardboard 23.5 cm (9¼ in) square and four pieces each 5.5 cm x 23.5 cm (2¼ in x 9¼ in). Insert a 5.5 cm x 23.5 cm (2¼ in x 9¼ in) piece of cardboard through the unstitched edge of the tray into each of the three side panels, and the square piece into the centre. Draw a square around the central piece, joining the four inner corners. Carefully stitch along this line between the pieces of cardboard (DIAGRAM 4).*

7. *Insert the fourth 5.5 cm x 23.5 cm (2¼ in x 9¼ in) piece of cardboard into the unstitched side. Fold in a 1 cm (⅜ in) seam allowance along the open edge and neatly hand-stitch closed.*

8. *Tie the ribbons into bows to bring together the sides of the tray. As the tray is completely reversible, this can be done with either fabric on the inside.*

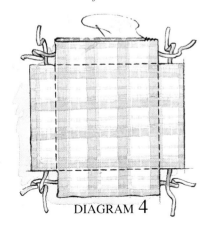

DIAGRAM 4

Wrapped in ribbons

Ring the changes by adding extra ribbons and bows to the basic pattern for the croissant tray.

MATERIALS & EQUIPMENT

You will need the same materials and equipment as for the tray on page 14, except that you will require 2.25 m (2½ yds) of 9 mm (⅜ in) ribbon in each of two different colours matching or contrasting with your fabric instead of 1.3 m (1½ yds).

1. *Cut each length of ribbon into four 55 cm (22 in) lengths. Cut out the two pieces of fabric for the tray, each 38 cm (15 in) square, then mark out a 6 cm (2¼ in) square on each corner (DIAGRAM 1) and cut away these squares.*

2. *On the right side of one piece of fabric, pin a length of ribbon 4 cm (1½ in) in from each long edge, and stitch these ribbons in place to within 1 cm (⅜ in) of the short edges of the fabric (DIAGRAM 2). Repeat with the other square of fabric and the remaining ribbons, but sew them 1.5 cm (⅝ in) in from the edge of the fabric.*

3. *Pin the two pieces of fabric to each other with right sides together, taking care to keep the ends of the ribbon lengths folded in towards the centre so that they do not get stitched into the seam. Machine-stitch the pieces of fabric together right around the tray with a 1 cm (⅜ in) seam, but leaving one end open.*

4. *Proceed as for STEPS 6-8 of the croissant tray, opposite.*

6 cm (2 in)

6 cm (2 in)

38 cm (15 in)

DIAGRAM 1

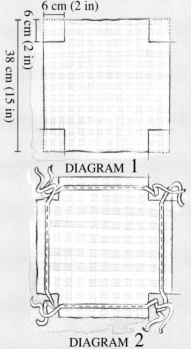

DIAGRAM 2

The floral arrangement

You don't have to be a professional florist to produce a pleasing floral arrangement. Grouping flowers, herbs and fruit informally in an assortment of containers can achieve just the look that is needed to complement your bright breakfast table.

FRUIT WITH FLOWERS

Create a bold display with wild flowers and fruit still on the branch in a clutter of mismatched mugs and jugs. Small fruits such as berries and kumquats are ideal for this kind of arrangement, but larger, colourful fruit such as oranges or lemons with their leaves on can be equally decorative – simply pile them onto a plate or arrange in a bowl.

THE SINGLE COLOUR DISPLAY

Colours that harmonise are easy to combine, yet they can produce a very effective display. Choose an assortment of flowers in shades of one colour and arrange them separately in a variety of tall and short coloured drinking glasses before grouping these together on the table.

SINGLE BLOOMS

Let individual flowers with distinctive shapes speak for themselves by placing single stems into separate containers such as simple glass bottles and grouping the containers together. Use both the height of the containers and the length of the flower stems give the arrangement form. If a large arrangement in the middle of your table is going to take up too much space, place a single small flower in a small container at each place setting.

FLOATING FLOWERS

Snip the heads off full blooms and float them in water in an assortment of glass bowls and dishes. To make a strong statement, use a single, large bloom in a bowl of a similar size, or float smaller flower heads together to create a massed effect. Extra colour can be introduced by tinting the water with food colouring, or by placing coloured glass marbles or chips in the water, and you can also add a subtle fragrance to the air by adding flavourings such as orange essence.

CHAPTER TWO

Down to earth

If you can't have lunch in the country, bring a touch of the countryside
to your home with a combination of hand-painted enamelware,
a checked tablecloth and a bunch of wild flowers. The aroma of
sweet-smelling herbs encased in muslin bags will help to create just the
right atmosphere for a casual meal with friends.

The enamelware

You can paint a design on enamelware as easily as you would on paper. Simple geometric designs are probably easiest to work with, but use your imagination or draw inspiration from an endless number of sources such as books, magazines and fabrics for the designs of your choice. You may find some enamelware in second-hand shops, or you could try camping stores for new, inexpensive enamelware.

MATERIALS & EQUIPMENT

◆ Enamel plates, mugs and a jug
◆ Craft paint suitable for metal surfaces, in the colours of your choice
◆ Paper and a sharp pencil
◆ Ruler, protractor, pair of compasses, masking tape, tracing paper, carbon paper and self-adhesive dots (all optional depending on your design)
◆ Medium and fine paintbrushes

THE PLATES

As it is easier to work on a flat surface than a curved one, start by working on the plates, then move on to the mugs and jugs when you are comfortable with the technique.

1. *Work out your design on paper first, using one of the plates as a template to draw the circle so that you can plan your design to the exact size.*

2. *If you wish to follow the design shown here, it is important to work out the pattern repeat of the wavy border, or you may end up with an awkward section where the end of the line does not join up neatly with the starting point. The easiest way to do this is to divide the circle into equal segments before you start drawing. Find the diameter of the circle by folding the paper in quarters; the point where the two folds meet is the centre of the circle. Place a protractor on the diameter line with its midpoint on the centre, and*

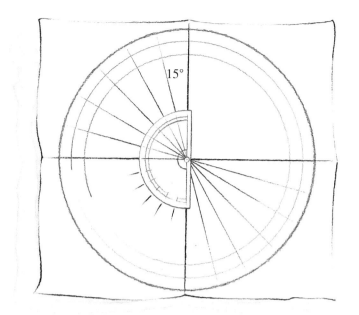

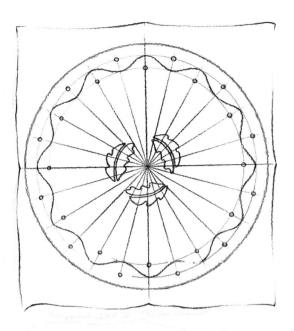

DIAGRAM 1

DIAGRAM 2

*divide the 360° of the circle into equal slices (*DIAGRAM 1*). The size of these slices will determine the size of your pattern. Large slices will result in a very shallow wave, small slices will give you a busier design. For an average dinner plate, 24 slices of 15° each will produce a pleasing pattern repeat.*

3. *Place the point of a pair of compasses in the centre of the circle and draw two concentric circles, 0.5 cm (³/₁₆ in) and 2.5 cm (1 in) in from the edge of the original circle. These will help you to draw waves of equal depth.*

4. *Carefully draw a continuous wavy line between these two circles, and draw*

*dots on either side of the line to coincide with the 15° lines (*DIAGRAM 2*).*

5. *Draw the leaf pattern on* PAGE 88 (TEMPLATE 2.1) *in the centre of the circle.*

6. *When you are satisfied with your rough design, you are ready to start painting the plate. Wipe the surface so that it is clean and free of dust. Transfer the leaf design onto the middle of the plate and the wavy line and dots onto the border with carbon paper (*PHOTO 1*). It may be easier to cut the centre out of the paper design if your plate is deep. If you prefer, use a pencil to draw the design onto the plate. Any mistakes can be rubbed off with a soft cloth.*

7. *Paint the wavy line, then add the dots with the end of the paintbrush (*PHOTO 2*). Finally paint in the leaves (*PHOTO 3*).*

THE MUGS AND JUG

Follow the same technique applied to the plates to paint the mugs and jug. If you want your mugs to match your plates, paint the wavy border and dots around the top, then apply scaled-down leaves randomly over the rest of the surface. There is no need to worry about the border's pattern repeat, as the line will be interrupted by the handle. Note that when working out the design on your jug, remember to scale up the pattern so that it is in proportion to the size of the jug.

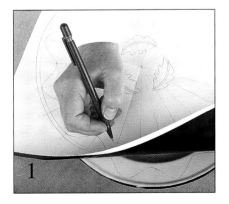

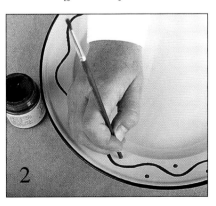

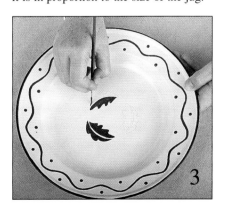

Mix-and-match crockery

If you stick to the same colours, there is no reason not to vary the designs for a mix-and-match set of mugs.

METHOD A

For a fun design, stick self-adhesive dots randomly over the surface of the mug. Make sure that they are well stuck down before applying paint in a ring around the dots; take care not to cover the dots, otherwise the paint may peel off as you lift them (PHOTO 1). When the paint is almost dry, carefully lift the edges of the stickers with the point of a craft knife and peel them off. Paint in the centre of the dots in the same colour or a contrasting colour, leaving a small gap between each dot and the ring of colour unpainted to edge the dots (PHOTO 2).

METHOD B

Use masking tape to mask off the top of the mug. Draw evenly spaced vertical lines in pencil and paint in alternate stripes in the colour of your choice (PHOTO 3). This can be done freehand, or you can use masking tape for neater edges. Carefully remove the masking tape while the paint is still wet so that the paint does not peel off with the tape. When the stripes have dried, paint in the wavy border and dots as you did for the plates.

METHOD C

As a really simple alternative, paint the whole mug in bold, vertical stripes, as described above but leaving off the wavy border and dots.

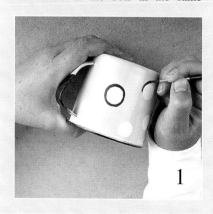

1

2

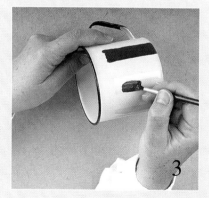

3

All tied up

Replace the conventional napkin ring with a few simple alternatives using inexpensive, easy-to-obtain materials such as raffia, corrugated cardboard, cotton string and fresh herbs.

M E T H O D   A   *(right)*

1. Cut nine lengths of raffia, each about 60 cm (24 in) long. Tie these together with a knot about 4 cm (1⅝ in) from one end. Divide the lengths into three lots of three and plait them to within 4 cm (1⅝ in) of the other end. Tie a knot to secure the plait.   2. Fold the napkin in half and roll it up lengthways. Wind the raffia plait around the roll three times and tie the ends into a knot.

M E T H O D   B   *(above)*

1. Cut a 5 cm x 15 cm (2 in x 6 in) rectangle of corrugated cardboard, its length running across the corrugations.   2. Roll up the napkin as described above.   3. Wrap the cardboard strip around the roll and tie a length of cotton string around it to hold it in place. Tie the ends into a neat bow.

M E T H O D   C   *(above)*

1. Cut a 4 cm (1¾ in) section from the cardboard core of a toilet roll or paper towel roll.   2. Stick the end of a length of raffia to the inside of the core with masking tape. Cover the entire core by winding raffia through the centre and around the outside. As raffia comes in quite short lengths, you will probably have to join several pieces; don't try to conceal the knots, as they add to the overall effect.   3. Stick the end of the raffia to the inside of the core with masking tape.

M E T H O D   D   *(below)*

1. Cut a rectangular piece of brown paper about 5 cm x 15 cm (2 in x 6 in).   2. Roll up the napkin as described in METHOD A *and wrap the paper strip around the roll. Hold this in place with a small piece of adhesive tape.   3. Drip sealing wax onto the adhesive tape to conceal it, and use a seal, ring or coin to make a decorative impression before the wax sets.*

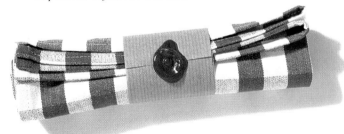

M E T H O D   E   *(below)*

1. Form a piece of florists' wire into a ring about 7 cm (2¾ in) in diameter. Roll up the napkin and slide the wire ring over.   2. Carefully wind cuttings of fresh herbs around the ring to conceal the wire and create a truly fresh herbal napkin ring. These rings must be prepared on the day they are to be used, as the herbs will wilt within hours of being cut.

Herb sachets

Muslin bags filled with aromatic herbs make inexpensive gifts for lunch guests and add a decorative touch to a rustic table setting. To dry herbs, hang bunches of them upside down in a protected, dry place for a week or so, or leave them in a warm oven for a few hours. When dry, crumble them to release their scent.

MATERIALS & EQUIPMENT

◆ Muslin cloth – one 30 cm (12 in) square per sachet for METHOD A or 30 cm x 10 cm (12 in x 4 in) per sachet for METHOD B
◆ 40 cm (16 in) jute string, raffia or ribbon for each sachet
◆ Assorted dried herbs
◆ Needle or sewing machine and cotton thread for METHOD B
◆ Safety pin or tapestry needle

METHOD A

1. *Cut a circular piece of muslin, using a plate with a diameter of 25 cm (10 in) as a template to mark out the circle.*

2. *Place a small handful of dried herbs in the centre of the circle.*

3. *Gather up the muslin around the herbs, and tie a length of ribbon, string or raffia into a knot around this. Tie the ends into a neat bow and fan the muslin out above this.*

METHOD B

1. *Fold the rectangle of muslin in half to form a 10 cm x 15 cm (4 in x 6 in) rectangle. Stitch a seam down each side to form a bag.*

2. *Turn the bag the right way round, then fold down the top 3 cm (1¼ in) of fabric towards the inside. Stitch down all the way round, 2.5 cm (1 in) from the folded top edge.*

3. *Form a casing for a drawstring by sewing a second row of stitching 1 cm*

(⅜ in) up from your first stitching line. Carefully unpick the side seam of the bag between the two rows of stitching to insert the ribbon.

4. *Using a safety pin or a needle with a large eye, thread a 30 cm (12 in) length of ribbon, string or raffia through the casing, leaving enough of a 'tail' on the outside to tie in a bow once the bag is drawn closed (PHOTO 1).*

5. *Fill the bag with dried herbs, pull the drawstrings and tie into a neat bow.*

The tablemats

In this reverse appliqué technique the leaf design is cut out of a piece of fabric to reveal a different fabric beneath. The richly contrasting colours used here were chosen to coordinate with the painted enamelware, but if you prefer more muted shades, try finding fabrics with contrasting textures or patterns instead.

MATERIALS & EQUIPMENT

FOR EACH TABLEMAT YOU WILL NEED:
- ◆ Two 45 cm x 32 cm (17 in x 13 in) pieces of red fabric
- ◆ One 45 cm x 32 cm (17 in x 13 in) piece of green cotton fabric
- ◆ Sewing thread to match the red fabric
- ◆ Dressmakers' carbon paper and tracing wheel
- ◆ Pins and a needle
- ◆ A sharp pair of scissors

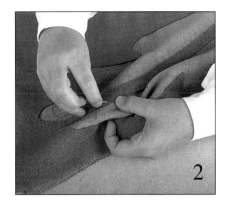

3. *Turn the cut edge of the leaf outline under by 1 cm (⅜ in) (along the dotted line), snipping the fabric where necessary, and hand-stitch the top piece of fabric to the bottom one with neat running stitches just inside the turned edge* (PHOTO 2).

4. *Lay the second piece of red fabric on top of the first piece (which is now attached to the green piece in the middle by the appliqué stitches). Pin all three layers together and stitch a 1 cm (⅜ in) seam around three and a half sides, leaving an opening large enough for the mat to be turned the right way out.*

5. *Trim the seam and turn the mat right side out through the unstitched opening* (PHOTO 3). *Press the seams flat and hand-stitch the opening closed.*

1. *Enlarge the leaf design on* PAGE 88 (TEMPLATE 2.2) *on a photocopier so that the leaf measures about 24 cm x 32 cm (10 in x 13 in). Transfer the design onto the centre of one piece of red fabric with a tracing wheel and dressmakers' carbon* (PHOTO 1).

2. *Cut out the leaf shape along the solid line. Pin the piece of red fabric to the green fabric and tack it down about 2.5 cm (1 in) from the edge of the design.*

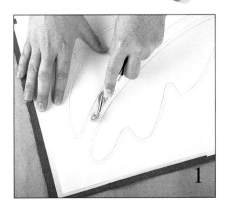

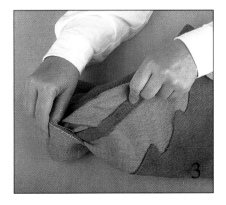

CHAPTER THREE

Tea for two

Teatime is a special time of indulgence, so take out your best china and lay it out on a table decked with the prettiest appliquéd tablemats and napkins, scone holder and jam jar. Strawberries and cream set the theme for the appliqué motifs and the hand-painted jam jar.

The tablemats

These floral tablemats are framed by a border of green checked fabric and decorated with an appliquéd strawberry in one corner. If you prefer a simpler look, use a checked fabric (such as gingham) in the centre and matching plain fabric for the border.

MATERIALS & EQUIPMENT

FOR EACH TABLEMAT YOU WILL NEED:

◆ 30 cm x 45 cm (12 in x 18 in) floral cotton fabric
◆ 40 cm x 55 cm (16 in x 22 in) green checked fabric to match the floral fabric
◆ Small pieces of red and green cotton fabric for the appliqué design
◆ 30 cm x 45 cm (12 in x 18 in) thin polyester wadding (batting) for quilting

◆ Iron-on interfacing
◆ Sewing thread to match your fabric
◆ White and black thread for the appliqué design
◆ Water-soluble fabric marker pen
◆ Ruler
◆ Sewing machine
◆ Sharp scissors
◆ Paper, tracing paper and pencil
◆ Needle and pins

1. *Lay the 40 cm x 55 cm (16 in x 22 in) piece of checked fabric on a flat surface. Use a water-soluble fabric marker pen and a ruler to mark a 30 cm x 45 cm (12 in x 18 in) rectangle in the centre of the piece of fabric, leaving a 5 cm (2 in) border all round (DIAGRAM 1).*

2. *Lay the rectangle of wadding (batting) onto this marked rectangle, and then the floral rectangle on top of this. Tack the layers together to hold them in place. Use the water-soluble pen and ruler to mark light diagonal lines, 5 cm (2 in) apart, across the fabric. Machine-stitch along these lines through all three layers (DIAGRAM 2).*

3. *Fold in each corner of the unquilted border of checked fabric diagonally, so that the middle of the diagonal fold meets the corner of the quilted section (DIAGRAM 3). Press the fold flat with an iron, then cut off the corner of the larger rectangle of fabric 5 mm (¼ in) in from the fold.*

4. *Fold in the flaps of the larger piece of material and stitch the diagonal seams neatly by hand (DIAGRAM 4). Tack the folded border in place, and finish by stitching the raw edge with a fine zigzag stitch through all thicknesses. If you wish, stitch a second row of zigzag stitches on the border 1.5 cm (⅝ in) from the first row.*

5. *To make the strawberries for the corner, trace the two components of the fruit design given on PAGE 88 (TEMPLATES 3.1 AND 3.2) and transfer onto paper. Carefully cut out these shapes to use as templates.*

6. *Cut a square of red fabric for the strawberry and green for the leaves, and press iron-on interfacing onto the back of each piece of fabric to stiffen it and make it easier to work with. Place the templates on the pieces of fabric and pin them in position. Carefully cut around the templates.*

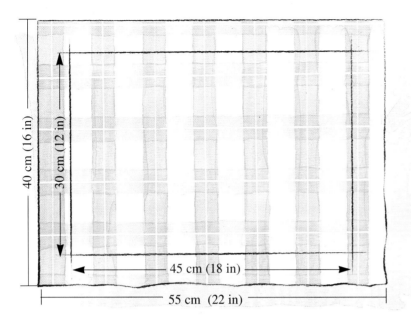

DIAGRAM 1

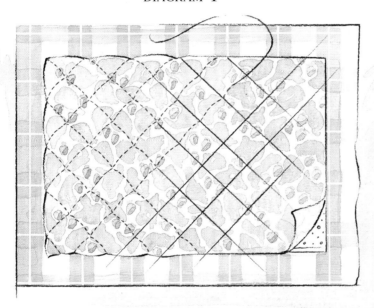

DIAGRAM 2

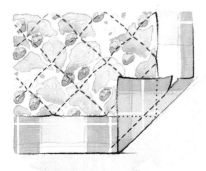

DIAGRAM 3

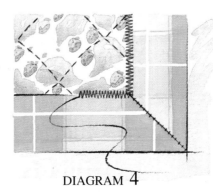

DIAGRAM 4

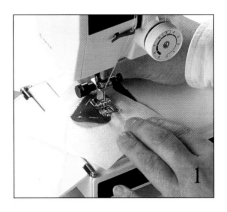

7. *Place the strawberry cutout on a piece of backing fabric a little larger than the berry and leaves, and tack it in position. Set your sewing machine to a fine zigzag stitch and thread it with white thread. Carefully stitch around the shape, sewing into every point and curve. Make sure that the edge of the motif is sewn, otherwise the fabric will soon fray around the stitching (*PHOTO 1*).*

8. *Position the cut-out leaf and stalk on top of the berry shape. Tack it in place and zigzag around the shape. Hand-stitch small, black dots on the strawberry and sew into the leaf shape with white thread, following the dotted lines on the leaf template on* PAGE 88 (TEMPLATE 3.2)*.*

9. *Carefully cut out the finished strawberry motif. Attach it neatly to one corner of the tablemat by stitching by hand from the underside of the mat so that the stitches are not seen on the surface (*PHOTO 2*). Make enough strawberries for one corner of each mat or, if you prefer, decorate all four corners on each mat.*

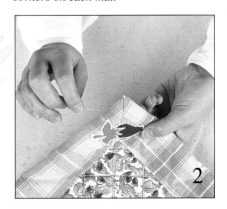

The napkins

These napkins coordinate with the tablemats to continue the strawberry theme, using a simplified version of the appliqué technique to decorate them.

MATERIALS & EQUIPMENT

FOR EACH NAPKIN YOU WILL NEED:

- 30 cm x 30 cm (12 in x 12 in) square of green checked fabric to match the tablemats
- 1.25 metres (1½ yds) narrow bias binding in a colour to match your fabric
- Sewing thread to match your fabric
- White and black thread
- Small pieces of red and green cotton fabric for the appliqué design
- Iron-on interfacing
- Sharp scissors
- Pins and needle
- Sewing machine
- Paper, tracing paper and pencil

1. *Round off the corners of the square of fabric. Open out one side of the bias binding and pin it all the way round the square, starting in the middle of one side. Stitch the binding down its fold line, easing it carefully around the corners.*

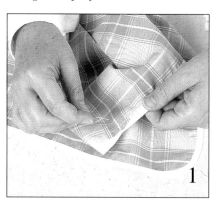

2. *Fold the binding over the raw edge of the fabric. Neatly slip-stitch it to the other side, overlapping the starting point by 1 cm (⅜ in) and tucking in the raw ends (PHOTO 1).*

3. *Photocopy the two components of the strawberry motif on PAGE 88, reducing their size if you wish. Cut out the shapes. Cut a square of red fabric for the berry and green fabric for the leaves. Press iron-on interfacing on the back to stiffen the fabric. Pin the templates to the pieces of fabric and carefully cut out the motifs.*

4. *Position the berry shape in one corner of the napkin, tack in place, then stitch down directly onto the napkin with a fine zigzag stitch (as in STEP 7 of the tablemat instructions). Finish by appliquéing the leaves (PHOTO 2), as described in STEP 8 of the tablemat instructions.*

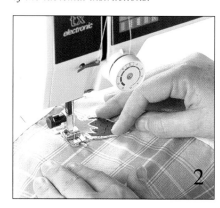

The jam jar

You can buy cold ceramic paints which are specially formulated for applying to glazed ceramics. These dry within a few hours and do not require firing in a kiln. Although they are for decorative rather than utilitarian use, so are unsuitable for plates, they are fine for painting a jam jar to match your table setting.

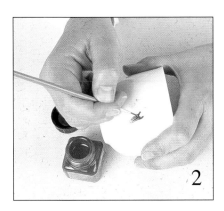

hold it in place with small pieces of masking tape. Draw over the design with a pencil to transfer it onto the jar (PHOTO 1). *Repeat the motif over the whole jar and lid. If you are not happy with any part of the design, simply wipe off the traced lines and redo the motif.*

3. *Starting with red, paint in the berries* (PHOTO 2). *When these are dry, paint in the green stalks and leaves and again leave to dry.*

4. *Finally, apply small dots to the strawberries with a cocktail stick and black paint* (PHOTO 3).

5. *When the paint is dry, bake according to the manufacturer's instructions.*

MATERIALS & EQUIPMENT

◆ A plain white, glazed ceramic jam jar – buy an inexpensive one from any shop that sells crockery
◆ Green, red and black ceramic paints (available at craft shops)
◆ Pencil
◆ Tracing paper
◆ Carbon paper
◆ Masking tape
◆ A fine paintbrush for painting the design, and a cocktail stick for painting in the dots

1. *Trace the whole strawberry design given on* PAGE 88 (TEMPLATE 3.3) *onto a small piece of tracing paper.*

2. *Cut a piece of carbon paper the same size as the tracing paper and place it on the jam jar, carbon-side down. Lay the tracing paper on the carbon paper and*

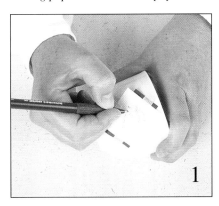

The scone holder

Match the fabric of the tablemats and napkins for this scone holder, which has eight pockets.
Alternatively, you may want to mix and match your own choice of fabrics; as long as you select fabrics
with harmonious colours, you can be assured of a successful end result.

MATERIALS & EQUIPMENT

- 30 cm x 90 cm (12 in x 36 in) each of floral and green checked cotton fabric to match the tablemats and napkins
- 30 cm x 30 cm (12 in x 12 in) polyester wadding (batting)
- 2.5 metres (2¾ yds) narrow bias binding in a colour to match your fabrics
- Sewing thread to match your fabrics
- Press studs

- 30 cm (12 in) ribbon, 9 mm (⅜ in) wide
- Round bread basket, 25 cm (10 in) in diameter
- Paper and pencil
- Scissors
- Pins and needle
- Sewing machine
- Water-soluble fabric marker pen
- A ruler

DIAGRAM 1

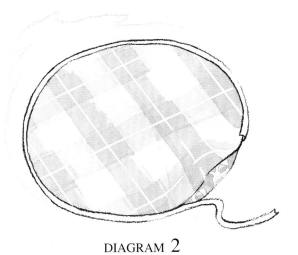

DIAGRAM 2

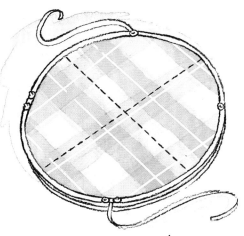

DIAGRAM 4

1. *Using a dinner plate as a guide, draw a circle 25 cm (10 in) in diameter on paper. Cut this out and use it as a pattern to cut two circles from each piece of fabric.*

2. *Take one circle of each fabric and pin them to each other with wrong sides together. Repeat with the other pair of circles. Bind each pair of circles with the bias binding. The neatest way of doing this is to open out one side of the binding and pin it around the edge of the circle, stitch it in place along the fold line of the binding (DIAGRAM 1), fold the binding over the raw edges of the fabric and neatly slip-stitch it in place (DIAGRAM 2).*

3. *Place one bound circle on top of the other with the checked fabric uppermost on both. Stitch these two circles together with two lines of stitching running*

through the centre of the circle at right angles to one another (DIAGRAM 3).

4. *Stitch the press-stud halves to the edge of the top circle as shown in DIAGRAM 4. Cut two 15 cm (6 in) lengths of ribbon and hand-stitch each piece to the edge of the top circle next to the press studs.*

5. *Cut a 27 cm (11 in) square from each of the fabrics and from the wadding (batting). Sandwich the wadding between the fabric squares, so that the right sides of the squares of fabric are facing outwards, and tack the layers together to hold them in place.*

6. *Using a water-soluble fabric pen and a ruler, lightly mark quilting lines, 5 cm (2 in) apart, in a criss-cross pattern on the fabric. Machine-stitch along the lines through all three layers of fabric.*

7. *Use your paper pattern to cut a circle from the quilted fabric. Neaten the edge with an overlock stitch and bind it with the bias binding, as described in STEP 2.*

8. *Lay the quilted circle on your working surface with the floral fabric uppermost. Lay the joined circles, with the checked fabric uppermost, on top of the quilted one. Pin the lower unquilted fabric circle to the quilted one, then carefully stitch these two together in the form of a cross, with the lines of stitching running between those that join the top two circles and as far in to the centre as you can go. Snap the press studs on the edges of the top circle together so that the fabric doesn't get in the way while you sew (DIAGRAM 5).*

9. *Neatly tie the ribbons into a bow and place the finished holder in the basket.*

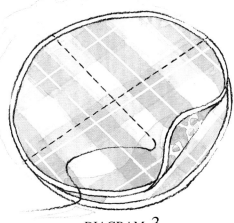

DIAGRAM 3

DIAGRAM 5

CHAPTER FOUR

Simply fishy

Get in tune with nature and set the scene for an outdoor meal, using
simple decorating techniques and some basic materials to deck out your table.
Create the mood of the seaside with a fish motif and carry the
theme through with pebbles and shells.

The tablemats and napkins

There are numerous ways of repeating a motif or pattern. For example, you can make a stencil,
as described in chapter 1, use carbon paper to transfer the design then paint it in, as described in chapter 2, or buy
a rubber stamp from a craft shop. Here an alternative technique, which is both simple and cost effective,
successfully combines a sponged-on motif with stencilling.

MATERIALS & EQUIPMENT

- ◆ A3 sheet of white paper
  for each tablemat
- ◆ Good quality white paper napkins
- ◆ Rope-coloured and
  blue acrylic paint
- ◆ Clear acetate film
- ◆ Sharp craft knife
- ◆ Fine-tipped permanent marker
- ◆ Pencil and ruler
- ◆ Masking tape
- ◆ Sponge
- ◆ Paper towel or newspaper

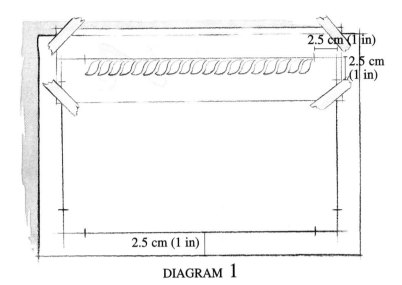

2.5 cm (1 in)

2.5 cm (1 in)

2.5 cm (1 in)

DIAGRAM 1

1. Start by making a stencil for the rope border. Cut a piece of acetate film 38 cm x 10 cm (15 in x 4 in) in size. Place this over the rope template on PAGE 89 and use a permanent marker to trace the design until you have drawn 32 cm (13 in) of 'rope'. Carefully cut out the design with a sharp craft knife.

2. Using a pencil and ruler, lightly draw a rectangle on the sheet of A3 paper, 2.5 cm (1 in) in from the edges. This will serve as a guide for positioning the edges of the stencil. Make a mark 2.5 cm (1 in) along the drawn lines from each corner of the rectangle to indicate where the strips of stencilled rope design should start and finish.

3. Position the stencil on the inside of the guide line and hold it in place with masking tape (DIAGRAM 1). To remove excess stickiness and prevent the tape from tearing the paper when the stencil is lifted, stick the tape onto a piece of fabric before applying it.

4. Pour a small quantity of rope-coloured paint into a saucer. Dip a small piece of sponge into the paint and dab off any excess on paper towel or newspaper. Very little paint is required and the sponge should be as dry as possible to prevent 'bleeding' under the edges of the stencil. Apply the paint to the cut-out area of the stencil with a dabbing motion (PHOTO 1).

5. Carefully remove the stencil and reposition it on one of the other sides. Stencil all four sides, masking off some of the cut stencil for the shorter sides. Set the paper aside while you prepare the fish and shell motifs.

6. Draw fish and starfish designs (TEMPLATES 4.2 AND 4.3 ON PAGE 89) onto a sponge with a felt-tipped pen. Cut out the designs with a craft knife (PHOTO 2).

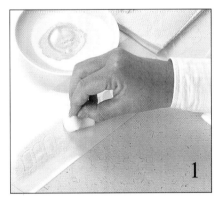

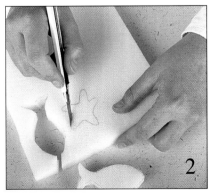

7. Starting with the starfish motif, dip the sponge into the same paint that you used for the rope border. Again dab off any excess and position the sponge in the corner of the border (see photo on PAGE 36). Press it lightly onto the paper, and repeat in the other three corners.

8. Fill in the centre of the tablemat with fish applied in the same way as the starfish, but using the blue paint (PHOTO 3). You could plan the positioning of each motif, but this is time-consuming and not really necessary, as a random scattering of fish produces a casual and far more pleasing result.

9. If you have access to a plastic laminating service (offered by speciality outlets), you may want to laminate your tablemats to preserve them. If not, the amount of time and money spent on the mats is minimal, so you can afford to throw them away after the meal and make more when you need them again.

10. Use either the shell sponge or the fish sponge to decorate one corner of each paper napkin (PHOTO 4).

The tray

A sponge technique similar to that used for the tablemats and napkins is used here to decorate a wooden tray. In this case, however, the fish motif is created by sponging on a number of small squares to give the design the appearance of an intricate mosaic.

MATERIALS & EQUIPMENT

◆ A rectangular wooden tray. If you can't find a plain one, you will need to get rid of as much of the paint or varnish as possible with paint stripper or sandpaper
◆ Wood primer
◆ White undercoat
◆ Light grey, black, white, blue and beige acrylic paints
◆ Clear varnish
◆ Paintbrushes
◆ Carbon paper
◆ Pencil
◆ Synthetic sponge
◆ Ruler
◆ Felt-tipped pen
◆ Sharp craft knife
◆ Paper towel or newspaper
◆ Soft, lint-free cloth

1. *Apply a coat of wood primer to the tray with a paintbrush and allow it to dry thoroughly.*

2. *Give the tray two good coats of white undercoat, allowing the paint to dry between coats. Then apply a coat of light grey paint to the upper surface of the base of the tray and allow to dry thoroughly (PHOTO 1).*

3. *Using a photocopier, enlarge the fish design (TEMPLATE 4.4) given on PAGE 89 until it fits comfortably into the base of your tray – there should be a gap of about 5-6 cm (2-2½ in) between the edges of the tray and the head and tail of the fish to allow space for the painted border and the background.*

4. *Lay a sheet of carbon paper, carbon-side down, on the tray and position the enlarged fish design on top. Draw over the design with a pencil to transfer it onto the tray.*

5. *Use a felt-tipped pen and ruler to mark out a few 13 mm (½ in) squares on the sponge, then cut these out with a sharp craft knife (PHOTO 2). These blocks will be used to apply paint in a way that will create a mosaic effect.*

6. *Place a small quantity of each of the black, blue, beige and white paint colours on a mixing tray. Dip a sponge block into the black paint, dab off any excess paint on a piece of paper towel or newspaper, and press the sponge onto the tray in a corner. Repeat in a line around all four sides, leaving small gaps in between each square as you would if you were working an actual mosaic (PHOTO 3). Work*

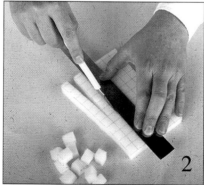

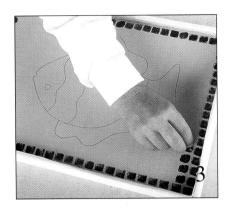

two rows in black, then fill in the rest of the area surrounding the fish design with squares of beige paint.

7. Outline the fish's body with a row of black squares, then fill in the body, tail and fins with blue and beige (PHOTO 4). Create a range of blues and beiges by

blending in touches of white to lighten them and black for darker shades. Try to avoid overlapping squares, although the fish shape will make this unavoidable in places. For really tricky bits, you could cut the sponge into smaller shapes. Make the fish's eye black and sponge in the surrounding area in white.

8. When the paint is completely dry, mix some white paint with about five times as much water. Rub this over the tray with a soft cloth to soften the lines and give the surface an aged look (PHOTO 5).

9. Seal the tray with two or three coats of varnish, allowing it to dry between coats.

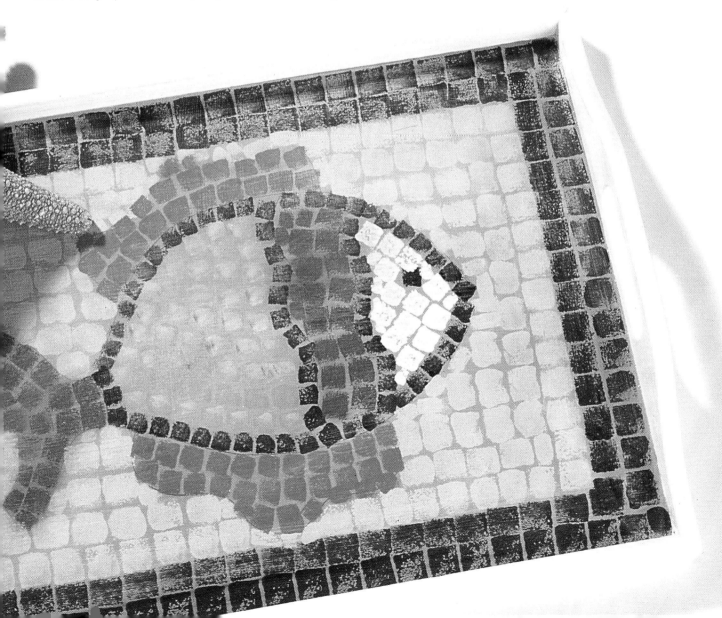

Shell details

You will need an assortment of shells for these projects. If you live near the sea, it is easy to collect them.
Otherwise ask a friend who does to send you some, or buy shells from a speciality store or gift shop.

THE TABLECLOTH

To weight your tablecloth down and prevent it from blowing away, sew individual shells along the edge of the cloth and clusters at the corners. Choose shells that are similar in shape or go for a mix-and-match look; just make sure that they are about the same size. Drill small holes through them, using a hand-drill with a small masonry bit, then sew them at regular intervals along the edge of the cloth with a strong thread. For the corners, choose larger shells and group them together.

THE NAPKIN TIES

Match the shell detail and stencilled rope border with some simple napkin ties to dress up your printed paper napkins. Cut a 35 cm (14 in) length of thin cotton rope. Tie a knot at either end, and sew a shell to each knot as you did along the hem of the tablecloth. Roll up your napkin or shape it into a loose cone by pinching it up at its centre point and shaking out the folds of the napkin, then tie the length of shell-decorated rope around it.

THE CANDLES

Floating candles are ideal for outdoors – simply float them below the rim of a bowl to protect the flame from the wind.

Melt plain white candles in an old double boiler or a large tin over simmering water, until the wax liquifies. If you want to make coloured candles, add wax colourant or pieces of wax crayon to the melting candles. Remove the wicks and set aside to re-use in the new candles. Pour the melted wax into plastic or metal shell-shaped moulds (available from cooks' speciality stores), or use half shells if available. Tie a small weight to one end of each wick, then insert a wick in the centre of each mould and suspend it until the wax sets. Trim the wicks, leaving about 1 cm (½ in) protruding from the top of each candle.

Ease the candles out of the moulds, or if you are using shells, let them remain in the shells. Place some washed pebbles and shells at the bottom of a glass bowl. Fill the bowl about three quarters full with water, and float the candles in it. If you wish, add a little food colouring to the water.

Frosted glassware

Creating the effect of etching on glass does not take any special talent or
expensive equipment – simply stencil your design on with vinyl contact plastic and glass etching fluid,
available from hardware stores or craft shops.

MATERIALS & EQUIPMENT

◆ Glasses
◆ Glass etching fluid
◆ Tracing paper and pencil
◆ Vinyl contact plastic
◆ A sharp craft knife
◆ A small paintbrush

1. *Photocopy the fish and/or starfish
designs on* PAGE 89 (TEMPLATES 4.2 AND
4.3), *reducing their size if you wish, and
transfer the design(s) onto small pieces
of contact plastic.*

2. *Cut out the shapes with a craft knife,
position the contact plastic on the
outside of a glass, then stick it in place
(*PHOTO 1*). Rub the plastic down well to
ensure that the etching fluid does not
'bleed' under the edges of the stencil.*

3. *Paint a layer of etching fluid onto the
exposed area (*PHOTO 2*). Leave it to dry
for a few minutes before removing the
contact paper and washing the glass.*

NOTE: If you cut out the stencil shapes
carefully, you could use the positive
shape of the same design to etch some
of the glasses.

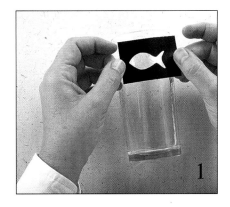

1

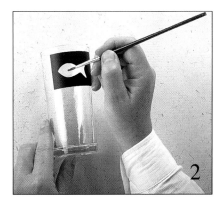

2

CHAPTER FIVE

Art on the table

A bright assortment of decorative products created predominantly from paper is combined with a collection of cheerful crockery and boldly coloured cutlery to set the mood for an informal dinner party. Try your hand at a papier-mâché bowl and napkin holders, decoupage tablemats and a bunch of paper poppies.

The bowl and napkin holders

Papier-mâché is not just for bored children on holiday — constructed carefully and imaginatively decorated, these table accessories will make an interesting and original feature on your table. Make a bold statement with simple geometric patterns and bright colours, or use the decoupage mats for inspiration.

MATERIALS & EQUIPMENT

- ◆ Newspaper
- ◆ Petroleum jelly
- ◆ Wallpaper paste
- ◆ Thin cardboard
- ◆ Masking tape
- ◆ White acrylic paint
- ◆ Gouache paints in the colours of your choice
- ◆ Non-toxic clear varnish
- ◆ Scissors
- ◆ Sharp craft knife
- ◆ Pencil
- ◆ Thick and thin paintbrushes

FOR THE BOWL YOU WILL ALSO NEED:
- ◆ A mould, such as a plastic or glass bowl, or a flat-topped metal lampshade; your choice will determine the shape of the finished product.

FOR THE NAPKIN HOLDERS YOU WILL ALSO NEED:
- ◆ Embroidery thread
- ◆ A piece of stiff card
- ◆ A sewing needle
- ◆ Two beads for each napkin holder

THE BOWL

1. Tear the newspaper into strips 10-15 cm (4-6 in) long and 2-4 cm (¾-1⅝ in) wide. Spread a thin layer of petroleum jelly over the outside of the mould.

2. Mix the wallpaper paste according to the instructions on the packet. Soak strips of paper in the paste and apply them to the mould, one layer at a time, extending them beyond the rim by about 2.5 cm (1 in) (PHOTO 1). Apply

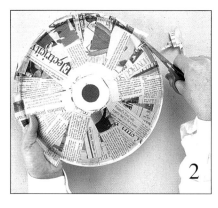

eight to ten layers, leaving each layer to dry before applying the next.

3. When the final layer of paper has dried completely, trim the top and bottom edges of the bowl with scissors (PHOTO 2). Insert a knife carefully between the mould and the papier-mâché shell to loosen and separate the two. Remove the hardened bowl from the mould and bind the top edge carefully with small strips of pasted paper to neaten it off.

4. Make a base for the bowl by cutting a circle of cardboard the same diameter as the bottom of the bowl and securing it to the outside with masking tape (PHOTO 3).

5. Apply two more layers of pasted strips to cover both the inside and the outside of the bowl, and leave to dry completely.

6. Paint the bowl with two coats of white paint to give it a smooth surface.

7. When the paint has dried, pencil your design lightly onto the painted surface. Fill in the design with gouache paints, starting with the lightest colour and working through to the darkest (PHOTO 4).

8. When thoroughly dry, seal the bowl with two layers of clear varnish.

THE NAPKIN HOLDERS

1. *Roll a 16 cm (6½ in) square of cardboard into a cone. Secure the join with masking tape. Cut the open end level so that the card is the size and shape of a large ice-cream cone (DIAGRAM 1).*

2. *Proceed as for the bowl, pasting small strips of paper onto the outside and over the top edge to the inside. Work carefully for the first couple of layers as you do not have a solid base to work on.*

3. *Paint the cone, following STEPS 6-8 of the bowl (opposite).*

4. *To make the tassels, wrap embroidery thread around a piece of stiff card cut as wide as the desired length of the tassels, until there is enough for the fullness you require. Secure the threads with a knot (DIAGRAM 2). Slide them off the card and wrap some more thread around them tightly, just below the top (DIAGRAM 3). Cut the loops of thread at the bottom.*

5. *Finally attach the tassel to the cone. Thread a needle with embroidery thread and knot the ends. Insert the needle through the top of the tassel, then through the eye of a bead and into the point of the cone. Bring the needle through a second bead on the inside of the cone, back*

through to the outside of the cone and again through the eye of the first bead (DIAGRAM 4). Pull the thread tight and secure it in the tassel, then trim the ends.

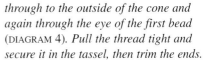

DIAGRAM **3**

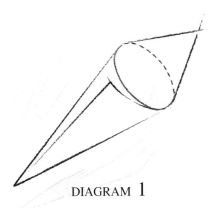

DIAGRAM **1**

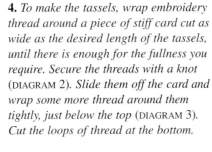

DIAGRAM **2**

DIAGRAM **4**

The tablemats

Decoupage is the application of decorative paper cutouts to a surface. Flat tablemats are ideally suited to this craft, and the design possibilities are endless, but if you want mats that are a nonstandard shape they may have to be specially cut. You can also use the technique to give old cork-backed mats a facelift. For the cutouts, choose suitable floral wrapping paper – the designs should have clearly defined outlines that will be easy to cut around.

1. *Paint the hardboard with wood primer. When dry, apply two coats of acrylic paint, allowing drying time between coats.*

2. *Cut out the flowers from the patterned paper with scissors or a craft knife. Lay the cutouts on the dry, painted surface of the mat. When you are happy with the arrangement, stick the paper cutouts down with glue, ensuring that each piece is firmly attached (PHOTO 1).*

3. *When dry, apply two to three coats of clear varnish to seal and protect the mat.*

4. *Stick felt to the back of the mat with glue (PHOTO 2), and when dry, carefully trim the edges of the felt.*

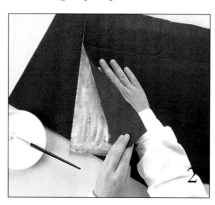

MATERIALS & EQUIPMENT

FOR EACH MAT YOU WILL NEED:

- 30 cm x 40 cm (12 in x 16 in) thin hardboard (masonite)
- Wood primer
- Acrylic paint in the colour of your choice
- Assorted pictures of flowers
- Clear varnish
- PVA glue
- Felt for backing
- Sharp craft scissors or craft knife
- Paintbrushes

Paper poppies

These cheerful paper poppies are so easy to make, and provide a colourful way to liven up any table setting.

M A T E R I A L S & E Q U I P M E N T

- ◆ Red crepe paper
- ◆ Black crepe paper
- ◆ Thick florists' wire
- ◆ Cotton wool
- ◆ Green florists' tape
- ◆ Thin florists' binding wire
- ◆ Sharp scissors or a craft knife
- ◆ Black pencil crayon

1. *Enlarge the petal pattern* (TEMPLATE 5.1 ON PAGE 90) *on a photocopier by 141% and transfer the shape onto the red crepe paper with the arrow on the diagram pointing in the direction of the*

grain of the paper. Cut out six petals with scissors or a craft knife; if you layer the crepe paper you will be able to cut out all six petals at once.

2. *If you wish, use a black pencil crayon to draw detail lines on each petal. Cup the petals by holding the centre of each*

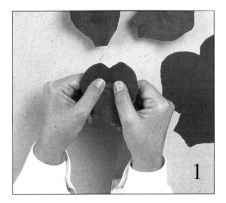

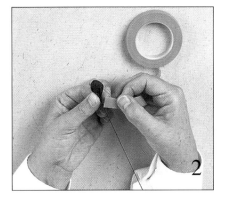

between your thumbs and forefingers and gently pushing and stretching the paper outwards to the sides (PHOTO 1).

3. *Cut a 2.5 cm x 20 cm (1 in x 8 in) strip of black crepe paper across the grain. Enlarge* TEMPLATE 5.2 *on* PAGE 90 *by 141% and use it to cut a 1 cm (⅜ in) fringe along one long edge.*

4. *Insert the end of a piece of thick florists' wire into the centre of a small ball of cotton wool. Cut a black crepe paper circle 6 cm (2¼ in) in diameter, wrap it around the cotton wool, and fasten it to the florists' wire (the stem) with tape* (PHOTO 2).

5. *Gather the black paper fringe in your fingers, wrap it around the covered centre, and secure it by wrapping thin binding wire around the stem* (PHOTO 3).

6. *Take the petals one at a time and gather the bottom edges, then cluster them around the poppy centre, overlapping them and securing them with thin florists' binding wire* (PHOTO 4).

7. *Working from the top of the stem, use green florists' tape to cover the base of the poppy centre and petals, and to wrap the entire stem* (PHOTO 5).

CHAPTER SIX

Putting on the glitz

Guests will be convinced that no expense has been spared in creating this lavish setting. But the clever use of fabric and a touch of gold proves that all that glitters need not cost a fortune.

The swagged tablecloth

A long undercloth in a subtle cream check is covered by a plain cream cloth, gathered up at intervals around the sides of the table to reveal the contrasting fabric. The edges of the top cloth are decorated with charming bunches of ivy and gold or cream bows at the gathers, providing a colourful accent and a counterpoint to the fruity centrepiece.

M A T E R I A L S & E Q U I P M E N T

◆ Two tablecloths in coordinating fabrics; the bottom cloth should be as long as possible, preferably down to the ground, and the top cloth must have a drop of at least 60 cm (24 in)

◆ Narrow curtain tape

◆ Cream sewing thread

◆ Gold or cream ribbon

◆ Sprigs of ivy and, if you wish, flowers and berries

◆ Thin florists' binding wire

◆ Gold spray paint

◆ Tape measure

◆ Ruler

◆ Water-soluble fabric marker pen

◆ Extra-long pins

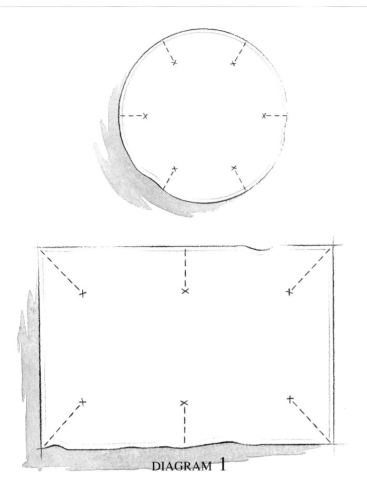

DIAGRAM 1

1. *Lay the top tablecloth upside down on your table, ensuring that the drop is even all the way round. If the table is square or rectangular, measure the sides and divide this measurement into equal parts of between 50 cm and 1 m (20 in and 40 in) each. Use a water-soluble fabric marker to mark these points at the edge of the table and the points where the cloth will drape over the corners of the table. If your cloth is round or oval, measure its circumference and divide this measurement equally.*

2. *Remove the cloth from the table and lay it out flat, again upside down. Draw lines from the marks to the edge of the cloth as shown in* DIAGRAM 1.

3. *Stitch lengths of narrow curtain tape along these lines* (PHOTO 1). *Tie a knot in the drawstrings at one end of the tape. Pulling the other end of the drawstrings, gather up each section tightly* (PHOTO 2). *Tie the long end of the drawstrings into a bow so that they can be undone when the cloth is washed.*

4. *Lay the bottom cloth on the table and top it with the swagged cloth. Tie bunches of ivy with the florists' wire* (PHOTO 3). *You can also include flowers or sprays of berries, but you will have to prepare these very close to the time when you need them, as the flowers will soon wilt if kept out of water. Lightly spray the ivy with gold paint so that the leaves are just touched with gold* (PHOTO 4).

5. *Wrap a length of ribbon around the ivy to cover the wire, and tie it into a generous bow. Use long pins to attach the bunches to the cloth between the swags at the edge of the table* (PHOTO 5).

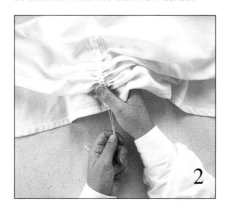

The chairs

These chair covers are very simple to assemble. They consist of two rectangles of fabric — preferably the same fabric as you used for the undercloth on the table — draped across each other over the chair and tied together with ribbons to hold them in place.

MATERIALS & EQUIPMENT

FOR EACH CHAIR YOU WILL NEED:
- A length of cream fabric to match your tablecloth (see Measuring the fabric, page 53)
- 3.75 metres (4 yds) gold or cream ribbon
- Water-soluble fabric marker pen
- Cream sewing thread
- Tape measure
- Pins

MEASURING THE FABRIC

*To calculate how much fabric you need for the first rectangle, measure from the floor to the top of the chair back and down to the seat, across the seat and down to the floor at the front of the chair (*DIAGRAM 1*). Add 2.5 cm (1 in) to each end for the hem. For the width of this rectangle, measure the width of the chair and add on 10 cm (4 in), that is, 5 cm (2 in) to prevent the chair from sticking out at the sides, and another 5 cm (2 in) for a 2.5 cm (1 in) hem on each side.*
*For the second rectangle, measure from the floor up to the side of the chair, across the seat and down the other side to the floor (*DIAGRAM 2*). Add 2.5 cm (1 in) to each end for the hem. For the width, measure from the back to the front of the chair seat, and add 2.5 cm (1 in) to each side for the hems.*

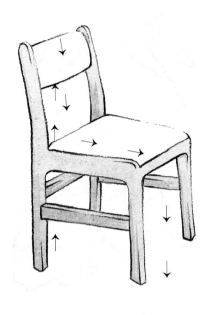

DIAGRAM 1

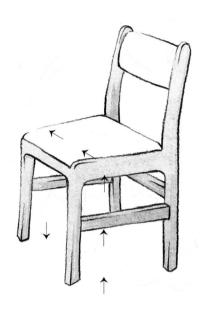

DIAGRAM 2

1. *Cut two rectangles of fabric to size according to your calculations. Stitch in 2.5 cm (1 in) hems round all four sides of each rectangle.*

2. *Drape the long rectangle over the length of the chair, and lay the smaller rectangle across the width. Using pins or a water-soluble fabric marker pen, mark the points where the pieces of*

fabric will be held together. The first two pairs of ribbons will tie the drop of cloth down the back of the chair (the longer piece of fabric) to the shorter piece of fabric where the seat meets the back of the chair. The second pair of ribbons will be tied at the front two corners of the chair, where the two pieces of fabric cross. The third pair will be tied half way up the back of the chair. Mark these

points on both pieces of fabric (you should make 12 marks – DIAGRAM 3*).*

3. *Remove the fabric from the chair. Cut the ribbon into twelve 30 cm (12 in) lengths, and stitch the lengths of ribbon in place, turning the raw ends under. Drape the fabric rectangles over the chair again and tie the ribbons into neat bows (*DIAGRAM 4*).*

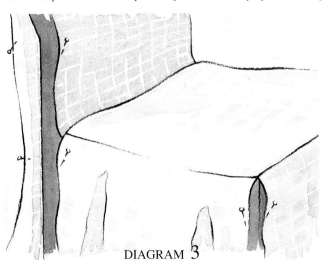

DIAGRAM 3

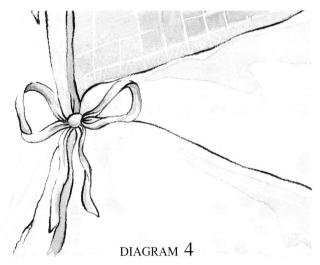

DIAGRAM 4

Folded napkins

Crisply starched napkins folded into a decorative shape are one of the details of a well-laid table that should not be overlooked. For each of these folding methods, you will need ironed, well-starched napkins. Keep a hot iron handy to press the napkins after each step to ensure that they maintain their shape perfectly.

PEACOCK

Lay a well-starched napkin, about 35 cm x 35 cm (14 in x 14 in) in size, out flat.

Concertina the entire napkin from edge to edge, forming six or seven pleats (PHOTO 1). Grasp the pleated napkin in the middle (PHOTO 2), and hold the pleats

in place by inserting the prongs of a fork into them. Fan out the folds prettily so that the arrangement stands up, resembling a peacock's tail (PHOTO 3).

SWALLOW

BIRD OF PARADISE

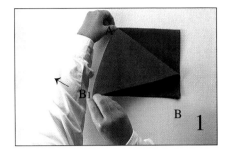

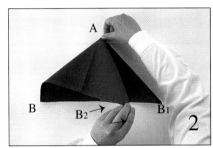

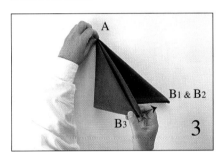

CORONET

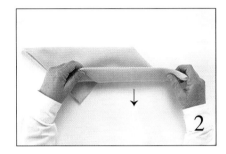

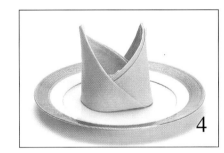

You will need a napkin which measures about 40 cm x 40 cm (16 in x 16 in). First lay it out flat, then fold it diagonally so that it forms a large triangle. Fold this triangle in half to form a smaller triangle (PHOTO 1). Concertina the whole napkin up from the base line to the top (right-angled) corner in three folds (PHOTO 2). Pinch the pleated napkin flat in the middle (PHOTO 3). Place a knife and fork here, criss-cross fashion, on the middle of the pleats so that the 'swallow's' wings stand up (PHOTO 4).

Lay a 40 cm (16 in) square napkin out flat then fold it in quarters. With one finger on point A, pull the top layer of fabric at B across to the left to form two unequal triangles (PHOTO 1). Turn the whole napkin over. Holding one finger on A again, pull the top layer of fabric at B (the bottom left corner), B2, across to B1 to form a triangle (PHOTO 2). Fold the napkin in half so that B3 meets B1 and B2 (PHOTO 3). Fan out the four points. If the napkin is well starched, you can stand the arrangement up (PHOTO 4); if not, lay it flat on plate.

Fold a 40 cm (16 in) square napkin in half. Bring the top right corner down to the midpoint of the bottom edge, then bring the bottom left corner up to the top edge (PHOTO 1). Turn the napkin over so that the two long sides are parallel to you. Fold the bottom edge up to the top edge, and pull out the flap lying underneath (PHOTO 2). Fold the right side of the napkin in half and tuck it under the left-hand flap (PHOTO 3). Turn the napkin over and tuck in the other side as before. Pick up the napkin and open out the base (PHOTO 4).

Fruity centrepiece

Instead of the usual floral arrangement, create this lovely autumnal
centrepiece, where berries and other fruit form colourful accents amid trailing greenery.

MATERIALS & EQUIPMENT

◆ Oasis

◆ Wire mesh

◆ A glass bowl on a stand

◆ Greenery (including trailing ivy),
fruit, berries and flowers in season,
and unshelled nuts

◆ Florists' wire

◆ Gold spray paint (optional)

1. *Immerse oasis in water. When it is
soaked through, wrap it in wire mesh
and place it in the bowl.*

2. *Insert sprigs of trailing ivy and other
greenery into the oasis (PHOTO 1).*

3. *Use florists' wire to bind the nuts into
clusters and to wire individual pieces of
fruit. Build up your arrangement with
the fruit, nut clusters and berries (if
available), allowing them to cascade
over the sides of the bowl (PHOTO 2).*

4. *Add a few elegant flowers such as
roses or lilies to fill out the arrangement
beautifully (PHOTO 3).*

5. *If you wish, spray parts of the finished
arrangement lightly with gold paint.*

The candle shades

These shaded candles will cast a warm light over your table without the glare of an open flame.
Candle carriers – the metal supports for the shades – fit neatly over the top of the candles.

MATERIALS & EQUIPMENT

- Candle carriers (available from decorating outlets)
- Brown paper or newsprint
- Handmade paper – an A2 sheet will make one shade
- Adhesive and double-sided tape
- Gold ribbon
- Brass split fasteners
- Ruler
- Pair of compasses
- Scissors
- Punch

1. First make a template for the shade from brown paper or newsprint. Measure the diameter of the top of the candle carrier, then draw two concentric circles with the compasses – the first a couple of centimetres larger than the diameter of the carrier and the second about four times the diameter of the first. Draw a straight line from the centre of the circle to any point on the circumference of the larger circle. Cut along this line, then cut along the circumference of each drawn circle (DIAGRAM 1).

2. Wrap the template around the candle carrier so that the ends overlap, and hold them in place with a small piece of adhesive tape (PHOTO 1). Mark the overlap, then remove the tape and flatten the paper. Trim the overlap to within 2.5 cm (1 in) of the marked line.

3. Lay the template on the handmade paper, trace around it, then carefully cut out the shape.

4. Punch holes at intervals of about 2 cm (¾ in) near the bottom edge of the shade.

5. Stick the shade together with double-sided tape. Insert brass paper fasteners down the join (PHOTO 2), thread narrow gold ribbon through the holes, binding the edge of the paper (PHOTO 3), and tie the ends in a bow.

6. Put your candle into a candlestick, press the carrier down onto the candle, then place the shade on top.

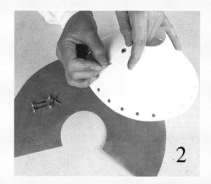

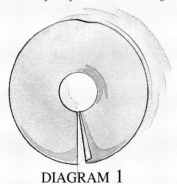
DIAGRAM 1

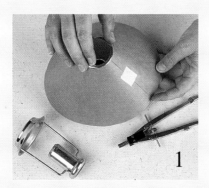

CHAPTER SEVEN

Party plan

It's a special occasion, so why not celebrate in style?
Choose a party theme with an elegant black and white colour scheme,
and carry it through from the invitations to the namecards
and menus, candle holders and gift boxes.

The invitations

Many stationery shops stock blank invitation cards, but creating your own personalised cards will set the tone for your party and give guests a hint of the theme you have chosen for the special night.

MATERIALS & EQUIPMENT

FOR EACH CARD YOU WILL NEED:
- ◆ One A5 sheet of thin black card
  - ◆ One A4 photocopied sheet of music
- ◆ One A5 sheet of onion skin or similarly textured fine paper
  - ◆ 40 cm (16 in) narrow silver ribbon
- ◆ Standard white envelopes
  - ◆ Silver sealing wax
    - ◆ Ruler
    - ◆ Craft knife
  - ◆ Paper glue (spray adhesive works well)
- ◆ Typewriter or fine-nibbed pen
  - ◆ Paper punch
  - ◆ Silver marker pen
- ◆ Ring, coin or embossed button

1. *First fold the A5 card in half. To do this neatly, measure exactly where the centre line lies and run a craft knife very lightly along this line. The knife must just score the surface of the card – take care not to cut through it. Fold the card then open it out flat again.*

2. *Apply paper glue or spray adhesive to the side of the card with the score line, and stick it to the back of the sheet of music-printed paper. Carefully cut off the excess paper around the card with a craft knife (PHOTO 1).*

3. *Fold the sheet of onion skin paper in half and trim 2 cm (¾ in) off the length and width of the folded rectangle. Type the wording of your invitation on the inner right-hand side, or use a fine-nibbed pen to write it out neatly.*

4. *Position the folded paper inside the card (PHOTO 2). Punch two holes in the spine through both outer and inner components, then thread a length of silver ribbon through the holes and tie it in a decorative bow.*

5. *When sending out the invitations, address the envelopes with a silver marker pen and seal the flaps with the silver sealing wax. If you don't have a seal, use a ring, coin or embossed button to make an impression in the sealing wax.*

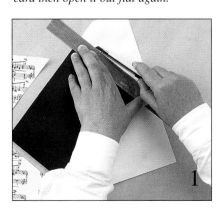

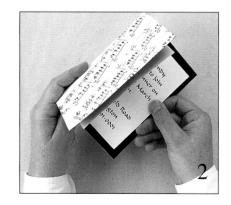

The candle holders

Place an arrangement of candles at the centre of the table and a single candle between pairs of place settings to create a magical atmosphere.

MATERIALS & EQUIPMENT

◆ White plastic plant pots – you will need a largish one for the centre of the table and small ones for the single candles
◆ Masking tape
◆ A block of polystyrene

◆ Sand
◆ An A4 and a few A3 photocopied sheets of music
◆ Double-sided tape
◆ Silver ribbon
◆ Large and small white candles

1. *Cover the hole at the bottom of each plant pot with masking tape. Wedge a block of polystyrene into the larger pot, making sure that it does not protrude above the top. (This will ensure that the pot does not become too heavy.) Pour sand over the polystyrene to cover it and to fill up any gaps in the pot. Fill the small pots with sand.*

2. *Stand each pot on the reverse side of a piece of photocopied paper in the middle of the sheet. Draw the paper up around the sides, holding it in place as you work with pieces of double-sided tape (PHOTO 1). When the paper is in place, wrap a ribbon around the top of the pot and tie the ends into a bow. Fan the edges of the paper out above the top of the pot. If the paper is not large enough to cover the plant pot generously, join two pieces together with adhesive tape on the reverse side.*

3. *Insert a group of white candles into the large pot, wedging them in the sand. A single smaller candle will suffice for each of the small pots.*

The napkins

Here is a very simple idea which will turn plain white napkins into a special and elegant finishing touch.

For each place setting, lay a napkin flat on the table, then fold it in half diagonally to form a large triangle. Roll this triangle up from the base to the point, and tie the roll into a loose knot. Before tightening the knot, insert the stem of a flower into the middle. Lay a napkin-wrapped flower on a plate at each place setting.

The namecards and menus

Personalised namecards on the table will show guests how much thought you have put into making them feel welcome. The method shown here involves printing each guest's name on a small piece of paper and inserting it into a decorated card with an attractive cut-out detail. The menus are created in a similar way, but the design is somewhat simplified.

MATERIALS & EQUIPMENT

◆ Thin black card

◆ Photocopied sheet music

◆ White paper

◆ 30 cm (12 in) narrow silver ribbon for each namecard or 40 cm (16 in) for each menu

◆ Tracing paper, pencil and ruler

◆ Craft knife

◆ Paper glue or spray adhesive

◆ Typewriter, wordprocessor, or fine-nibbed pen

◆ Paper punch

THE NAMECARDS

1. *Trace* TEMPLATE 7.1 *on* PAGE 90 *onto a piece of tracing paper.*

2. *Cut out a 10 cm (4 in) square from the black card. Apply paper glue or spray adhesive to the card and stick the card to the back of the music paper. Trim any excess music paper around the card with a craft knife.*

3. *Transfer the design you have traced onto the music-printed side of the card. Lightly score along the score lines (the dotted lines on the template on* PAGE 90).

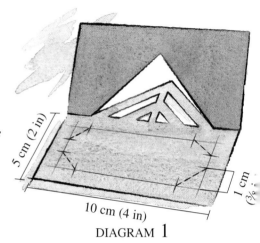

5 cm (2 in)
10 cm (4 in)
1 cm (⅜ in)

DIAGRAM 1

4. *Carefully cut along the lines of the design with a craft knife, then fold the card along the score lines so that the design stands up.*

5. *Cut a rectangle 7 cm x 2 cm (2¾ in x ¾ in) in size from the white paper. Type a guest's name across the piece of paper with a typewriter or a wordprocessor, or write it out neatly with a fine-nibbed pen or silver marker pen.*

6. *Cut out a piece of black card, 8 cm x 3 cm (3¼ in x 1¼ in) in size. Stick the name to the centre.*

MENU
Avocado Mousse

Grilled salmon
Baby potatoes
Minted peas
Greek salad

ELAINE

LAUREN

7. *Flatten the cut-out card, then draw a rectangle, 8 cm x 3 cm (3¼ in x 1¼ in) in size and 1 cm (⅜ in) in from the three edges, on the plain side of the half that will be the front of the finished card (DIAGRAM 1).*

8. *Mark points on each line 1 cm (⅜ in) from the corners. Draw a diagonal line across each corner connecting these points, and cut along the diagonal lines with a sharp craft knife (DIAGRAM 1). Insert the corners of one of the printed cards into these slits (PHOTO 1).*

9. *Thread a ribbon through the stand-up design and tie the ends into a neat bow.*

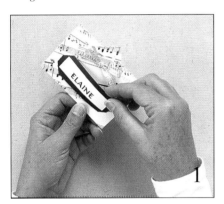

THE MENUS

1. *Cut an A4 sheet of black card in half lengthwise to make two menus. Lightly score a line across the middle of each card with a craft knife.*

2. *Stick music paper onto the side with the score line, then trim any excess. Fold the card along the score line.*

3. *Print your menu on a piece of white paper 9.5 cm x 7 cm (3¾ in x 2¾ in) in size, and stick it onto an 11 cm x 8.5 cm (4¼ in x 3¼ in) piece of black card.*

4. *Mark the folded card and cut slits in it as you did in STEPS 7 and 8 of the namecards. Insert the corners of the printed menu in the slits.*

5. *Punch two holes just below the folded top edge of the menu, thread a ribbon through them and tie the ends into a bow.*

Little boxes

Give guests an inexpensive gift such as sugared almonds or a couple of home-made chocolates in a special box that they can take home as a memento of a special evening. Place the boxes on the table next to each namecard. Here are two designs for you to choose from.

MATERIALS & EQUIPMENT

- One A4 sheet of thick card for BOX A, or one A3 sheet for BOX B to make a template
- One A4 sheet of thin white card for BOX A, or one A3 sheet for BOX B
- One A4 photocopied sheet of music for BOX A, or one A3 sheet for BOX B
- 70 cm (¾ yd) narrow silver ribbon for BOX A, or 30 cm (12 in) for BOX B
- Tracing paper and pencil
- Craft knife
- Ruler
- Paper glue or spray adhesive

1. *Enlarge the design of BOX A on PAGE 90 or BOX B on PAGE 91 by 141% on a photocopier. Transfer the shape onto the thick card, and cut it out with a craft knife. Use this as a template to mark out the boxes on thin card (PHOTO 1). Carefully score along the fold lines (indicated on the template with dotted lines) with a craft knife, ensuring that you don't cut through the card. Cut out the shape of the box.*

2. *Apply paper glue or spray adhesive to the side of the card with the score lines (PHOTO 2), and stick the card to the back of the sheet of music-printed paper. Use a craft knife to cut off the excess paper around the box shape.*

3. *Make up the boxes by folding along the score lines (PHOTO 3) and gluing if necessary. Insert your gift, and tie with a ribbon (see opposite page).*

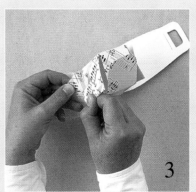

CHAPTER EIGHT

Dinner by candlelight

Weave a secret message of love into a clever heart-shaped card to set the scene
for a romantic Valentine's Day dinner. Follow through with red roses wrapped in
tulle, colour-coordinated tablemats and cloth napkins, and heart-painted champagne
glasses and candle shades. Stay with the traditional red and white,
and add the occasional accent of gold for a special touch.

The tablecloth

Loosely cover a tablecloth with a layer of white tulle.
You can play it safe with the ever-romantic white on white, or
try a traditional Valentine red on white or white on red. Scatter
red rose petals between the folds of tulle.

Painted glasses

Propose a toast to your
loved one with these elegant,
hand-painted glasses.

MATERIALS & EQUIPMENT

◆ Champagne glasses
◆ Gold outline glass paint
◆ Red glass paint
◆ Tracing paper and pencil
◆ Adhesive tape
◆ A fine paintbrush

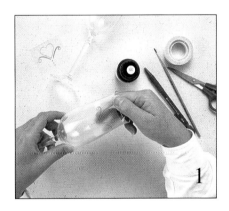

1. *Trace the heart and swirl design on*
PAGE 92 (TEMPLATE 8.2) *onto a small*
piece of tracing paper, then tape it in
position inside the glass (PHOTO 1).

2. *Paint in the swirls and the outline of*
the heart with the gold paint. When it is
dry, paint the heart in red (PHOTO 2).

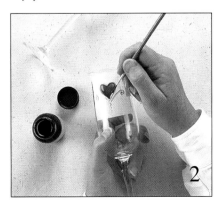

The napkins

Smart white napkins with a red border and back are given
a whimsical finish by the addition of four heart-shaped red buttons.
As they are decorative in themselves, the napkins can simply
be folded in quarters and placed on a side-plate.

MATERIALS & EQUIPMENT

FOR EACH NAPKIN YOU WILL NEED:

◆ 40 cm (16 in) square of
red cotton fabric
◆ 35 cm (14 in) square of
white cotton fabric
◆ Red and white sewing thread
◆ Four red, heart-shaped buttons
(if you can't find heart-shaped
ones, use round ones)

◆ Tape measure
◆ Sewing machine
◆ Iron
◆ Scissors
◆ Tailors' chalk or
a water-soluble fabric
marker pen
◆ Pins

1. *Make up a 35 cm (14 in) square*
red napkin by sewing a 2.5 cm (1 in)
hem all round the red fabric.

2. *Press a 2.5 cm (1 in) hem all round*
the white fabric, but do not stitch.
Trim the folded hem to 5 mm (¼ in).

3. *Measure 2.5 cm (1 in) in from all*
four edges of the red square and mark
out this inner square with tailors'
chalk or a fabric marker pen. Pin the
white fabric to the red, using the
marked lines as a guide (PHOTO 1).

4. *Feed white thread through the*
needle of a sewing machine and fill

the bobbin with red thread. Stitch
the white square to the red square
just inside the edge of the white
fabric. If your sewing machine's
tension is correctly set, the stitching
lines will be almost invisible, with
white stitches on the white fabric
and red stitches on the red fabric.

5. *Find the centre of the napkin by*
folding it into quarters. Using red
thread, stitch four small, red buttons
around the centre on the creases
(PHOTO 2). *Apart from adding a*
decorative touch, the buttons will
secure the red and white sections
of the napkin to each other.

The tablemats

Easy to make, these mats consist of a pretty paper doily stuck down onto a red cardboard or hardboard base. If you wish to varnish the mats, be sure to use good quality doilies and a spray varnish.

M A T E R I A L S & E Q U I P M E N T

FOR EACH MAT YOU WILL NEED:

- ◆ Thick cardboard or hardboard (masonite) cut into a circle 32 cm (13 in) in diameter
- ◆ Red acrylic paint or a piece of red card at least 32 cm (13 in) square
- ◆ A good quality round, white, paper doily, 20-25 cm (8-10 in) in diameter
- ◆ Spray adhesive
- ◆ Craft knife (if red card is used)

1. *Paint one side of each cardboard or hardboard circle with two coats of red acrylic paint, and allow this to dry between coats. Alternatively, spray adhesive on the red card, stick it to the circle and trim the edges.*

2. *Apply spray adhesive to the backs of the doilies. Carefully position*

them in the centre of the red circles and stick them down.

NOTE: Coasters for glasses can be made in the same way, using small cocktail-size doilies stuck onto cardboard circles with a diameter 3 cm (1¼ in) greater than that of the doilies.

Cards of love

The cards consist of two pieces interwoven to form a heart shape. They can be purely decorative, or you can conceal a short message of love within the woven strips. For an interesting texture, try using hand-made paper.

M A T E R I A L S & E Q U I P M E N T

- ◆ A4 sheet each of firm red and white paper
- ◆ 20 cm (8 in) gold or white ribbon
- ◆ 280 cm x 50 cm (110 in x 20 in) white tulle (optional)
- ◆ Pencil and ruler
- ◆ Sharp scissors or a craft knife
- ◆ A fine-nibbed pen or calligraphy pen
- ◆ Paper punch

1. *Following* TEMPLATE 8.1 *on* PAGE 92, *mark out one half of the card on each sheet of paper. You can scale the size up or down to suit your requirements – if you work according to the template, the finished heart will be about 13 cm (5 in) across and be made of 1 cm (⅜ in) squares; larger 2 cm (¾ in) squares will make a 20 cm (8 in) heart. Cut out the shape with scissors or a craft knife.*

1

2. *Measure and draw the cutting lines from the bottom (straight) edge to points in line with the start of the curve, as shown in the template. Carefully cut along these lines* (PHOTO 1).

3. *Lay the pieces of paper at right angles to one another and weave the strips in and out to form the checked heart* (PHOTO 2).

4. *To plan your secret message, lightly mark on the white card with a pencil where the strips overlap and pull the two halves apart again. Write your message in the marked areas* (PHOTO 3) *and then reweave the heart to conceal it.*

5. *Although the card will hold together without it, a ribbon adds a decorative touch and also enables the heart to be*

hung. Punch a hole through both pieces of paper just below the right angle at the top of the heart. Fold the ribbon in half, thread the loop through the hole and secure the ribbon by pulling the cut ends of the ribbon through the loop (PHOTO 4).

6. *If you wish, tie a large tulle bow around the backs of both chairs and hang a heart from the centre of each.*

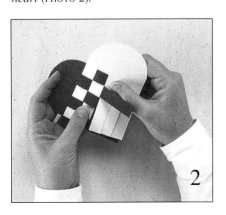

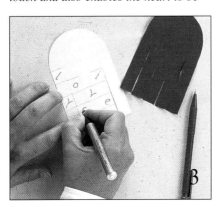

The floral arrangement

Long-stemmed red roses are the essence of romance. Instead of the usual arrangement in a vase, though, these roses are set in a shallow container and held together by a large, white tulle bow, to coordinate with the tablecloth and chairs.

1. *Cut the oasis down to size with a serrated knife to make it fit snugly into the basket or container.*

2. *Strip the rose stems of all their leaves except those just below the flowers. Carefully lay the flowers out in a row on your working surface and trim the stems with secateurs so that they are all the same length.*

3. *Insert the roses into the oasis one at a time, so that they stand upright (*PHOTO 1*). Start at the centre and work outwards until the oasis is well covered and the arrangement full.*

4. *Wrap the piece of tulle around the stems (*PHOTO 2*) and tie the ends into a large bow.*

MATERIALS & EQUIPMENT

- ◆ Oasis
- ◆ A small, shallow, white basket lined with plastic, or a porcelain container such as a casserole, about 20 cm (8 in) in diameter
- ◆ 20 straight-stemmed red roses
- ◆ 280 cm x 50 cm (110 in x 20 in) white tulle
- ◆ A serrated knife
- ◆ Secateurs

The candle holders and shades

Turn the lights down low and let candlelight create the romantic atmosphere needed for a special Valentine's Day dinner. A glass lampshade is easily converted into a candle holder with a base made of play dough.

M A T E R I A L S & E Q U I P M E N T

FOR THE SHADE YOU WILL NEED:

◆ A glass lampshade
◆ Gold outline glass paint
◆ Red glass paint
◆ Tracing paper and pencil
◆ Adhesive tape
◆ A fine paintbrush

FOR THE BASE YOU WILL NEED:

◆ 1 cup flour
◆ ½ cup salt
◆ 2 teaspoons cream of tartar
◆ 1 tablespoon cooking oil
◆ 1 cup boiling water
◆ Gold spray paint
◆ Red heart-shaped beads or rhinestones
◆ A saucer
◆ Clear adhesive glue

1. *Paint the glass lampshade, following the instructions given on* PAGE 67 *for the champagne glasses. Repeat the heart motif* (TEMPLATE 8.2 *on* PAGE 92) *at random over the entire surface, leaving off the swirls, and paint a ring of gold dots around the wide opening of the shade.*

2. *To form the base, mix the flour, salt, cream of tartar, oil and boiling water together to form a smooth dough. Although the dough will harden within a matter of hours, it should remain reasonably pliable for a few weeks if kept in an airtight container. Fill the saucer with the dough, pushing it down and smoothing over the top until it is level* (PHOTO 1). *Leave the dough for a couple of hours to harden.*

3. *Gently ease the dough from the saucer and turn it onto its flat side. Mark the centre point – just a visual estimate will suffice. Using the edge of the small opening on the glass shade, cut a hole in the centre so that there is a circular support exactly the right size for the shade* (PHOTO 2). *Leave the dough in a warm, dry place to harden further.*

4. *Spray the dough base with gold spray paint. When the paint is dry, stick beads or rhinestones around the base with clear adhesive glue* (PHOTO 3).

5. *Stand the glass shade in the base and place a tall, red candle in the centre.*

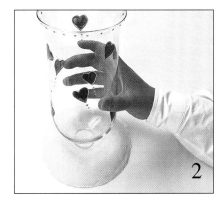

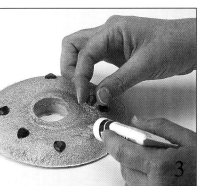

CHAPTER NINE

Christmas dinner

Take a break from the traditional colours of Christmas and deck out the table in crisp white with a sprinkling of golden stars and leaves. And don't pack away these decorations immediately after Christmas – they are sure to turn any meal into a special occasion.

Starry cloth and napkins

Spread a galaxy of stars across your dining table with this gold-printed, snowy white cloth,
and echo the theme at each table setting with a starry napkin.

M A T E R I A L S & E Q U I P M E N T

◆ White tablecloth
(If you do not have a tablecloth, refer to *The basic cloth* on page 11
for instructions on how to make your own)
◆ Napkins
◆ Gold fabric paint
◆ Tracing paper and pencil
◆ A large, firm potato
◆ A sharp knife

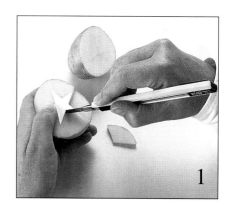

1

1. *Trace the larger star design on* PAGE 92; *cut out the shape. Cut the potato in half and position the template on the cut surface. Carefully cut around the design with a knife, so that the star stands out by about 5 mm (¼ in) (*PHOTO 1*).*

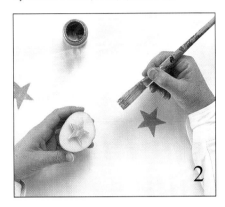

2. *Practise printing on a piece of scrap fabric before working on your cloth. Mix the fabric paint well, then apply it to the potato with a paintbrush (*PHOTO 2*) and press the potato down onto the scrap of fabric. Fresh paint must be applied after each print. When you are satisfied with the results, start printing the stars onto your cloth. A random sprinkling of stars is very effective, but if you wish to achieve a more formal look, mark out the position of the stars before starting.*

3. *Cut a smaller star on the other half of the potato and print the napkins in the same way.*

4. *Set your iron at the maximum temperature suggested for the material and iron on the reverse side of the cloth to fix the paint, going over each star for about three minutes (*PHOTO 3*).*

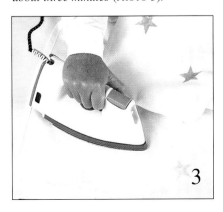

The napkin rings

These golden cherubs, made from moulded plaster of Paris, are a perfect addition to your Christmas table setting.

MATERIALS & EQUIPMENT

◆ Moulding plaster, such as plaster of Paris
◆ Large, brass curtain rings
◆ Gold spray paint
◆ A mould – the kind used for moulding chocolates works well

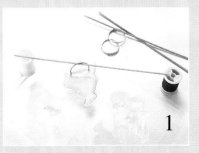

1. *Mix moulding plaster with water until it has a custard-like consistency. Fill the mould and insert a curtain ring so that the join is just below the surface (*PHOTO 1*). You will have to support the ring for a few minutes until the plaster starts to harden.*

2. *When the plaster is hard – after about 15 minutes – carefully ease it out of the mould and leave it in a warm place to dry out completely.*

3. *Spray the front and back of the napkin ring with gold paint (*PHOTO 2*).*

The underplates

These golden, leaf-rimmed underplates are not meant to function as tablemats,
but rather as decorative frames for the dinner plates.

MATERIALS&EQUIPMENT

FOR EACH UNDERPLATE YOU WILL NEED:

◆ Several ivy leaves
◆ Square of thick cardboard at least 25 cm (10 in) across
◆ Contact adhesive
◆ Gold spray paint
◆ Absorbent paper
◆ A pair of compasses

1. *As the leaves must be pressed, you will need to prepare them several days in advance. Place them between sheets of absorbent paper in thick books, ensuring that the leaves do not overlap each other (PHOTO 1). After a few days they should be nice and flat.*

2. *Draw a circle about 25 cm (10 in) in diameter on the cardboard and cut it out carefully with a craft knife. ·*

3. *Lay the leaves loosely on the edge of the cardboard circle so that they overlap each other and conceal the cardboard*

circle's edge. When you are happy with the arrangement, stick the leaves one by one to the cardboard (PHOTO 2).

4. *When the glue has set, spray the cardboard and leaves with a good coat of gold paint (PHOTO 3).*

Christmas crackers

No Christmas party is complete without crackers. Make your own to match your gold and white table setting, and choose a special little gift to insert for each person at the meal.

MATERIALS & EQUIPMENT

FOR EACH CRACKER YOU WILL NEED:

◆ A piece of firm white paper (not too thick) or starry wrapping paper, measuring 18 cm x 35 cm (7 in x 14 in)
◆ Three pieces of thin card for the inner tubes, each measuring 8 cm x 15 cm (3¼ in x 6 in)
◆ Thin cord or ribbon
◆ Paper glue or double-sided tape
◆ Self-adhesive stars for decoration (if plain paper is used)
◆ A small gift
◆ A cracker pull (if available)

1. *Roll up the three pieces of card for the inner tubes to a diameter of 5 cm (2 in). Overlap the ends and stick them together with tape or glue.*

2. *Stick the three tubes along the bottom edge of the paper rectangle, with the middle tube centred and the outer tubes 1.5 cm (⅝ in) in from either side of the paper (PHOTO 1). Insert a gift and cracker pull. Roll*

the paper tightly around the card tubes and secure the overlapping edge with glue or small pieces of double-sided tape.

3. *Tie a piece of cord or ribbon between the central and outer cores and squeeze gently, taking care not to tear the paper (PHOTO 2). Repeat for the other end. Decorate the cracker with self-adhesive stars if necessary.*

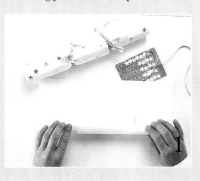

Topiary tree

There are two ways to prepare a 'topiary tree' centrepiece. The first is to plant ivy in a pot and train it around a wire shape. The disadvantage of this method is that you will need literally months to achieve the desired effect; on the other hand, you will have a permanent 'tree' which, if properly trimmed, will look good for years. The second, 'instant' method, shown here, involves winding cuttings of trailing ivy around a wire shape. Of course, the ivy will start to wilt after a day or two, so the 'tree' should be prepared on the day you want to use it.

MATERIALS & EQUIPMENT

- ◆ White crepe paper
- ◆ Plastic plant pot
- ◆ Masking tape
- ◆ Gold ribbon
- ◆ Potting soil
- ◆ Wire that is sturdy yet pliable (a wire coat hanger is ideal)
- ◆ Ivy plant or ivy cuttings
- ◆ Pebbles or polystyrene balls
- ◆ Gold spray paint (optional)

1. *Pleat a length of crepe paper and use it to cover the pot (PHOTO 1). Secure the paper to the bottom and inside of the pot with masking tape. Wrap a length of ribbon around the neck of the pot and tie the ends in a bow. Fill the pot with soil.*

2. *Bend the wire into the shape of your choice. You may choose to stick to the conventional Christmas tree shape, or try a heart, star or circle. Leave a long, straight piece at the base to anchor the wire. Insert this into the soil and make sure that the structure is sturdy.*

3. *If you are following the first method mentioned, plant the ivy in the pot and wind the stem around the wire; as the plant grows, gently train it to follow the shape of the wire. If you are taking the 'instant tree' route, simply twist lengths of ivy around the wire until you have a well-covered, bushy effect (PHOTO 2).*

4. *Cover the soil with pebbles, or with small polystyrene balls or chips that have been sprayed with gold paint.*

Decorated candles and leafy wreath

A handful of gold pins will transform plain white candles into elegant table decorations. Make your design as simple or as complex as you like, and if you like an ornate or colourful effect, try using sequins instead of pins.

MATERIALS & EQUIPMENT

◆ White candles
in a range of sizes
◆ Gold map tacks, or gold sequins
or beads and short pins
◆ Thick wire (such as a coathanger)
◆ Fronds of ivy
◆ Gold spray paint
◆ White plate
◆ Paper, ruler and pencil
◆ Adhesive tape

1. *Measure the height of each candle. Cut strips of paper as wide as each candle is high. Wrap a strip of paper around each candle and draw a pencil line to mark the overlap. Remove the paper from the candle and cut along the pencil line. The paper should now fit around the candle exactly.*

2. *Lay the paper flat and draw a design to indicate the positioning of the tacks or sequins. You may wish to create a grid for a geometric arrangement, or draw a shape such as a star.*

3. *When you are happy with your design, wrap the paper around the candle and hold it in place with a piece of tape. Push map tacks into the candle on the marked points shown on the paper or, if you are using sequins or beads, insert a straight pin through the centre of each sequin or bead and into the candle (PHOTO 1).*

4. *When you have studded all the points, carefully tear away the paper (PHOTO 2).*

5. *To make the wreath, bend the wire to form a circle just smaller than the plate, twist lengths of ivy round the*

wire until it is well covered (as for the Topiary tree, opposite), then spray the wreath with gold paint.

6. *Group the candles on a white plate and position the gold-leafed wreath around them.*

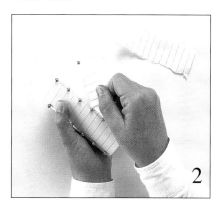

CHAPTER TEN

Child's play

For a tiny tot's birthday party, you can't beat a really bright table setting.
Put your child to work to devise a vibrant 'show of hands' with a tablecloth that
is literally hand-painted. Then turn sheets of coloured card into masks, 'dice' boxes
to fill with sweets, and embellishments for the straws, and finally
construct a balloon-filled centrepiece for a real lift-off.

The tablecloth

Prints made by hands dipped in paints of various colours create wonderfully spontaneous designs that will delight the little ones. If you don't have a cloth that you are happy to paint on, use an old sheet or make a cloth out of the cheapest fabric you can find. Refer to *The basic cloth* on page 11 for instructions on how to make a square, rectangular or round tablecloth.

MATERIALS & EQUIPMENT

APART FROM A PAIR OF EAGER LITTLE HANDS, YOU WILL NEED:

◆ A white cotton cloth
◆ Fabric paint in an assortment of bright colours
◆ Glass jars or foil baking trays (one for each colour of paint)
◆ Newsprint
◆ A large paintbrush
◆ Permanent black fabric marker pen

1. *Pour a small quantity of fabric paint into separate jars or foil trays. If the paint is too thick, use water to thin it down to the consistency of single cream. Prepare all the colours, even though you will work with only one at a time.*

2. *It is a good idea to practise the printing on a scrap of fabric first in order to establish just how much paint and pressure is required to produce a pleasing print. Cover a large, flat surface with newsprint and lay the scrap fabric on top of it. Starting with one colour, dip the paintbrush into one of the jars of paint and apply a coat to the palm and fingers of your child's hand (PHOTO 1).*

The hand is then pressed onto the cloth to transfer the paint. You will need to reapply the paint after each impression and keep each coat of paint as thin as

1

possible – if you try to save time by applying a thick coat or dipping the hands into the paint to make a few impressions before having to reapply, you will probably end up with some very blurred and blotchy prints.

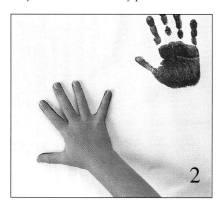

3. *When you and your child have mastered the technique, spread the cloth onto the newspapers and start printing. Space the prints far apart in a random fashion, until you are satisfied that there is adequate coverage of the first colour on the entire cloth* (PHOTO 2).

4. *Wash the paintbrush and your child's hands well before proceeding with the next colour. Continue working through all the colours until the cloth is well covered.*

5. *When the paint is completely dry, press the cloth on the reverse side with a very hot iron to fix the paint.*

6. *Finally, use a black fabric marker to draw dots for eyes and a curved line for a smiling mouth on the palm of each printed hand* (PHOTO 3).

The straws

Hold hands and smile... follow the theme of the tablecloth with these delightful junior 'cocktail' straws. The hands are simply cut from coloured card and wrapped around flexible straws.

MATERIALS & EQUIPMENT

- ◆ Coloured card to match the handprints on the tablecloth
- ◆ Flexible plastic drinking straws
- ◆ Tracing paper and a pencil
- ◆ Scissors or a craft knife
- ◆ Black felt-tipped pen
- ◆ Double-sided tape

1. *Trace the hand design on* PAGE 93 *and transfer it onto the coloured card, making a pair of hands for each straw.*

2. *Cut out the shapes, cut two slits as indicated, and draw in a pair of eyes and a mouth on the palms of the hands with a black pen, as for the tablecloth.*

3. *Take each pair of hands and stick a small piece of double-sided tape onto the strip of paper between the two hands. This will hold the card in place. Wrap each pair of hands around a straw and slide the two small slits into one another to join the hands together.*

The dice

Many children's games involve throwing dice. Give each child a giant dice that is actually a lucky-dip box filled with sweets. You could even devise a couple of games that involve playing with the dice during the party. Although those shown here have been made from coloured card, you could opt for the more traditional — and dramatic — black cube with white spots.

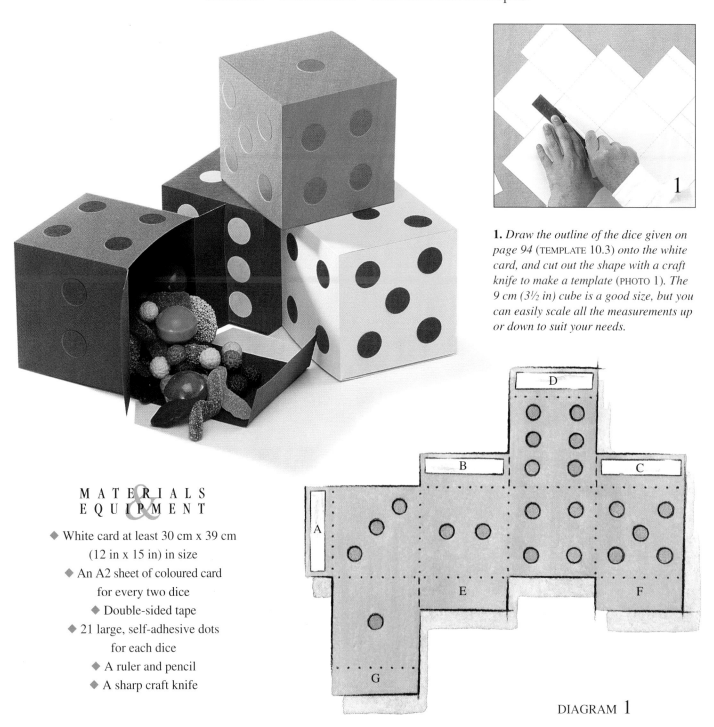

1. *Draw the outline of the dice given on page 94* (TEMPLATE 10.3) *onto the white card, and cut out the shape with a craft knife to make a template* (PHOTO 1). *The 9 cm (3½ in) cube is a good size, but you can easily scale all the measurements up or down to suit your needs.*

M A T E R I A L S & E Q U I P M E N T

◆ White card at least 30 cm x 39 cm (12 in x 15 in) in size
◆ An A2 sheet of coloured card for every two dice
◆ Double-sided tape
◆ 21 large, self-adhesive dots for each dice
◆ A ruler and pencil
◆ A sharp craft knife

DIAGRAM 1

2. *Use the template to mark out all the boxes on the coloured card, and cut them out with a craft knife.*

3. *Score all the fold lines by lightly running the blade of your craft knife along them. Take care not to cut all the way through the card.*

4. *Mark out the position of the dots on the same side as the score lines, as indicated on* DIAGRAM 1, *and stick the self-adhesive dots in place* (PHOTO 2).

5. *Stick a strip of double-sided tape on flap A as indicated on* DIAGRAM 1. *Start making up the boxes by folding along the scored lines and sticking flap A to the inside edge of the side with five dots on it* (PHOTO 3).

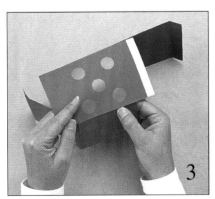

6. *Fold in flaps B and C and the side with six dots on it and stick them down. Then stick flap D to the inside of the side with three dots on it. Fill the box with sweets. Finally, fold in flaps E and F and close the lid (the side with one dot) by tucking flap G into the side marked with four dots.*

The masks

Turn coloured card into fun masks by cutting out a basic shape and decorating it with bright self-adhesive dots. If you are feeling creative, design your own mask shape and adorn it with sequins, beads, ribbons and whatever other materials you think will look good.

MATERIALS & EQUIPMENT

◆ Coloured card – you will need a rectangle about 21 cm x 7 cm (8½ in x 3 in) in size for each mask
◆ Coloured self-adhesive dots
◆ Hat elastic
◆ Tracing paper or carbon paper
◆ A pencil
◆ Scissors and a sharp craft knife
◆ A darning needle or a sturdy cocktail stick

1. *Copy the mask shape given on* PAGE 93 (TEMPLATE 10.2), *reducing its size if necessary, and transfer it onto the piece of coloured card using tracing paper or carbon paper. Alternatively, create your own designs and draw them onto the card.*

2. *Cut out the outline with scissors and the eye holes with a craft knife.*

3. *Decorate the mask with the self-adhesive dots.*

4. *Using a darning needle or cocktail stick, make a small hole on either side in line with the eyes. Thread a length of elastic through these holes and tie a knot at each hole to hold it in place.*

The centrepiece

A fountain of smiley-faced balloons and coloured napkins spills out of a paper bag to create a bright and cheerful focal point to the party table. The paper bag featured here is relatively simple to make, and is also perfect for holding gifts — especially oddly shaped objects that are awkward to wrap. Just scale the measurements up or down to produce the appropriate size for your table centrepiece or for gifts.

MATERIALS & EQUIPMENT

- ◆ A 64 cm x 35 cm (25 in x 14 in) sheet of white card
- ◆ A small quantity of two of the paint colours used for printing the tablecloth
- ◆ Double-sided tape
- ◆ 19 cm x 10 cm (7½ in x 4 in) piece of stiff card
- ◆ 70 cm (28 in) thin, brightly coloured nylon or cotton rope
- ◆ Balloons in assorted colours – 10 for the centrepiece and 3 for the back of each chair
- ◆ String and/or balloon sticks
- ◆ Coloured paper napkins
- ◆ Pencil and ruler
- ◆ A sharp craft knife
- ◆ A large paintbrush
- ◆ Paper punch
- ◆ A black felt-tipped pen
- ◆ Helium canister (if available)

1. *Lay the card on a flat surface. Mark out the score lines with a pencil and ruler (SEE TEMPLATE 10.4 ON PAGE 95). Run a craft knife lightly along these lines, scoring the dashed lines on the inside of the card and the dot-and-dash lines on the outside.*

2. *Fold over 3 cm (1¼ in) along the top edge and 2 cm (¾ in) along the left-hand edge towards the side of the card that will become the inside of the bag, as shown in the template.*

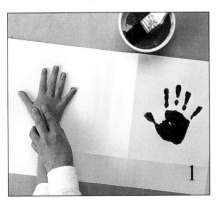

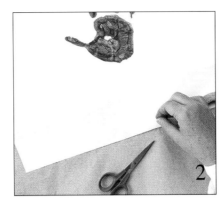

3. *Print two hands on the card as shown in* PHOTO 1, *using one colour for each side and following the method used to print the tablecloth. Draw a smiling face on each handprint with a felt-tipped pen.*

4. *Stick the short edges of the bag together with double-sided tape. Stick a piece of double-sided tape along the inside bottom edge of the paper, as shown in the template and* PHOTO 2.

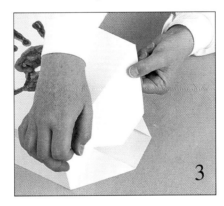

5. *Fold the card along the score lines so that the bag begins to take shape – as though you were wrapping a rectangular present (*PHOTO 3).

6. *Remove the backing from the double-sided tape and stick the bag together, then stick the piece of stiff card inside the bottom of the bag for stability.*

7. *Punch two holes for each handle along each of the bag's two long top edges.*

8. *Cut the length of rope in half. Thread each piece of rope through the punched holes and knot the ends on the inside so that handles are formed (*PHOTO 4).

9. *Inflate a batch of colourful balloons. If possible, fill them with helium so that they don't droop. (Helium canisters can be hired from a specialist hiring company, or you can buy ready-inflated balloons from a professional party planner.) Tie a length of string to each balloon. If you can't get hold of helium, fill the balloons with air and either use short pieces of string to prevent them from drooping, or attach the balloons to balloon sticks, which hold them upright. Use a black felt-tipped pen with a broad nib to draw a smiling face on each balloon.*

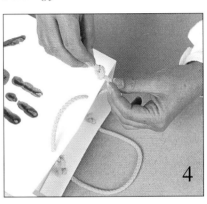

10. *Stand the completed bag in the centre of the table. Place a heavy weight such as a thick book or half a brick in the bag. Anchor the strings of the balloons under the weight so that the balloons float about 30 cm (12 in) above the top of the bag. Fill the opening of the bag with at least one paper napkin of each colour. Lay each napkin out flat, then pinch it at the centre point between a thumb and forefinger and use your other hand to flute it gently. Insert the centre point into the bag so that the corners fan out prettily at the top (*PHOTO 5).

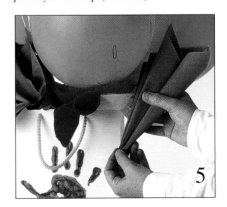

2 . 1

5 0 %

2 . 2

3 . 1

3 . 2

3 . 3

4 . 1

4 . 2

4 . 3

6 0 %

4 . 4

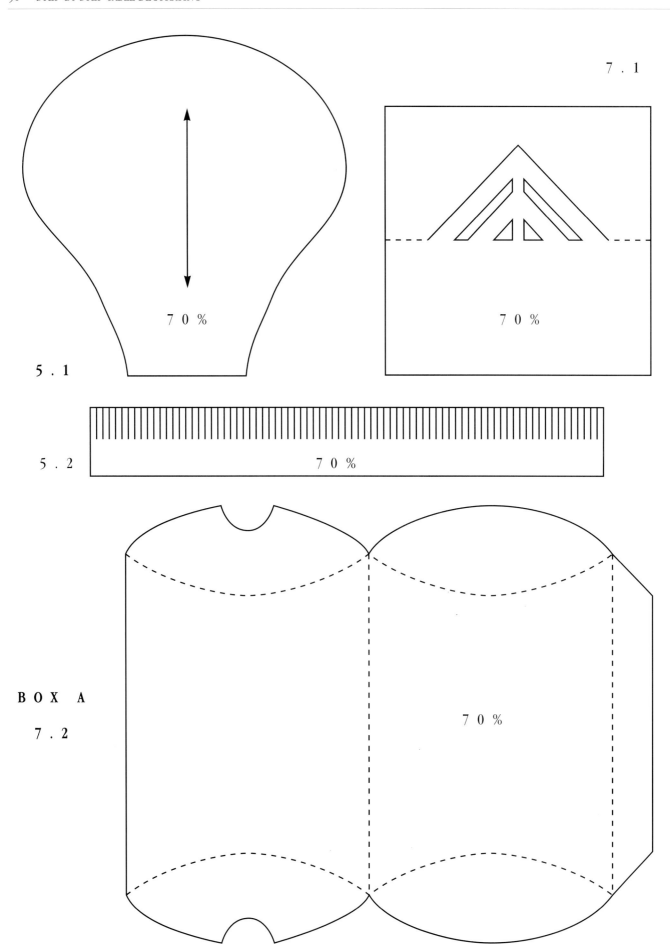

7 . 1

7 0 %

7 0 %

5 . 1

5 . 2   7 0 %

B O X   A

7 . 2   7 0 %

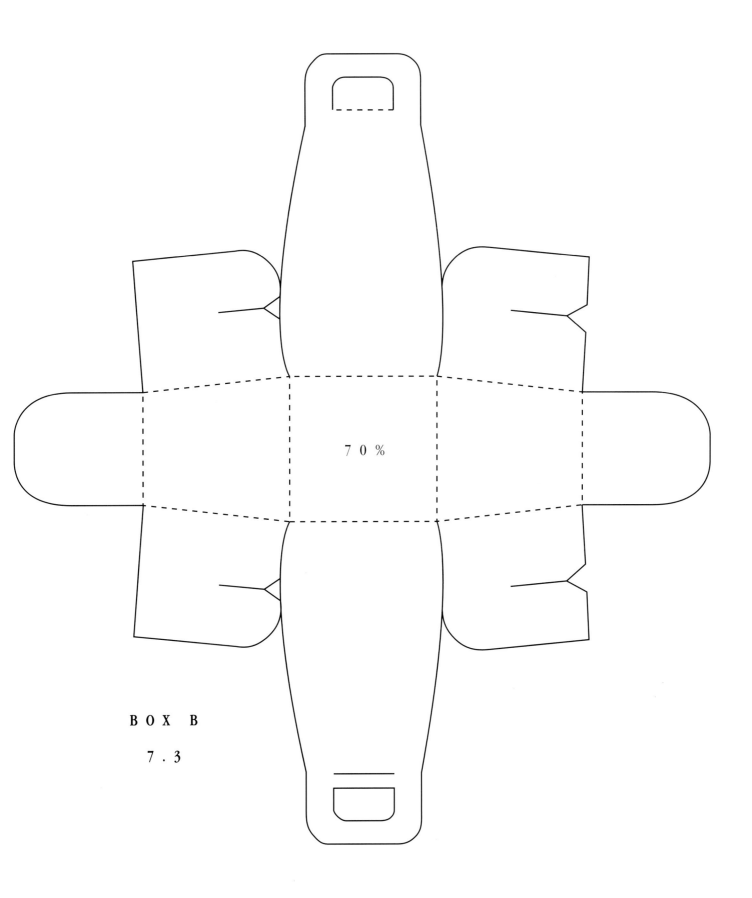

70 %

BOX B

7 . 3

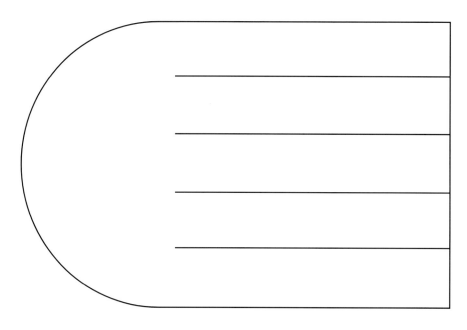

8 . 1

9 . 1

8 . 2

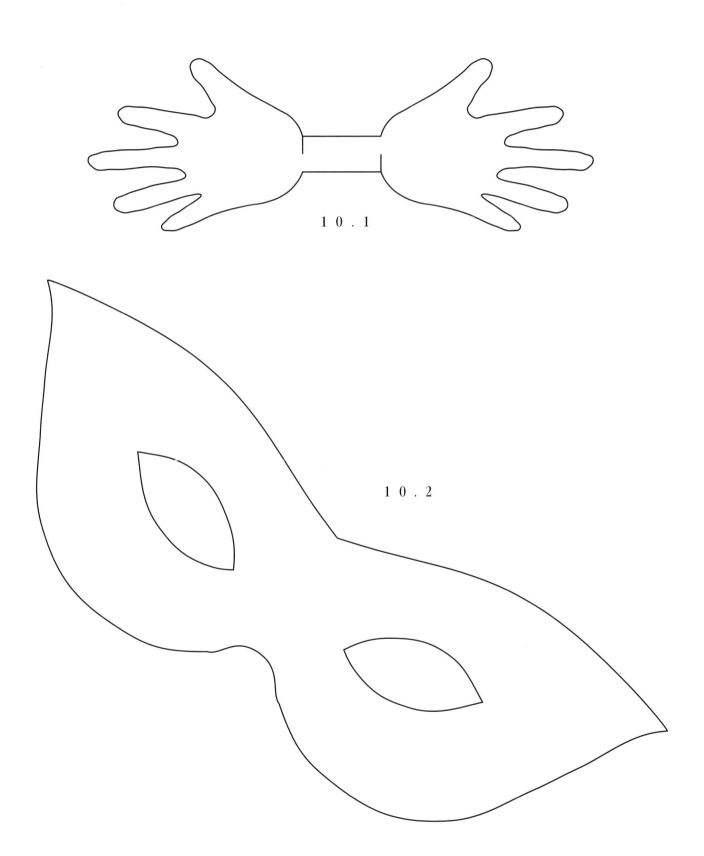

10 . 1

10 . 2

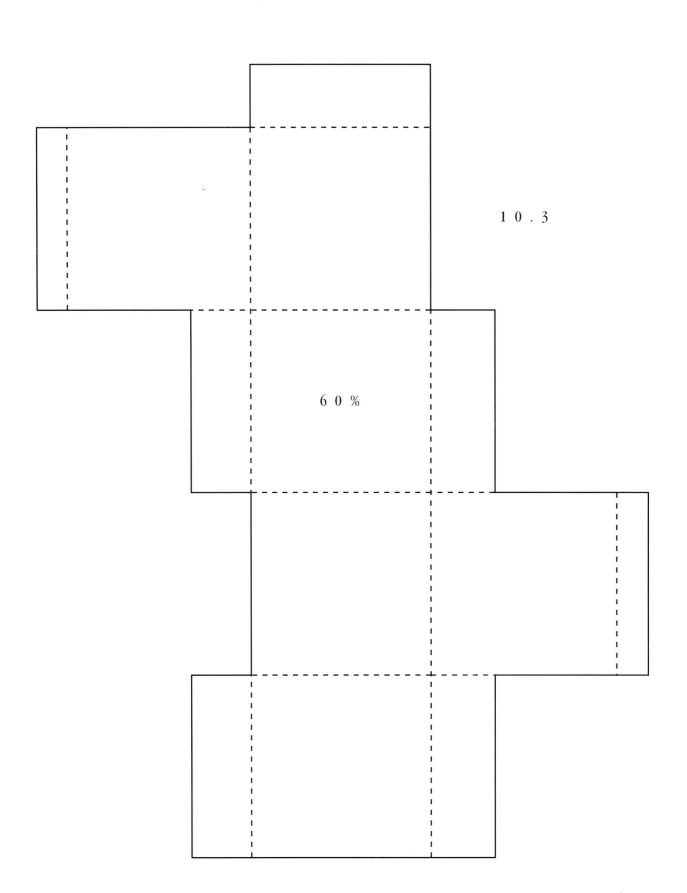

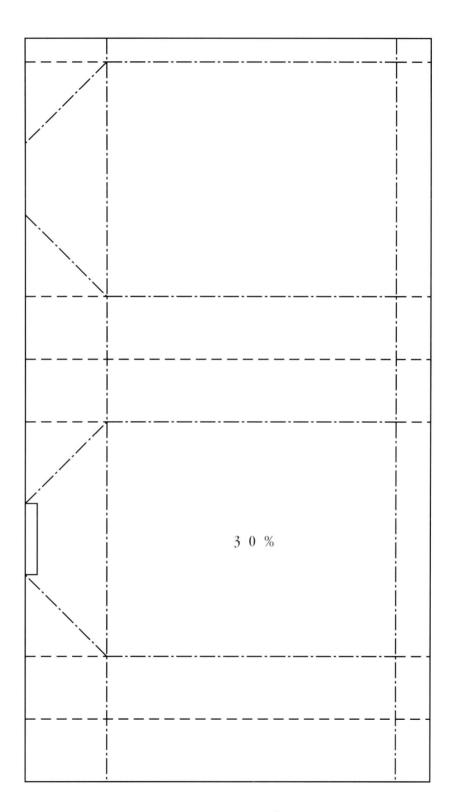

30%

10.4

96 •

I N D E X

This edition published in 1996 by New Holland (Publishers) Ltd
London ● Cape Town ● Sydney ● Singapore

24 Nutford Place, London W1H 6DQ, United Kingdom
Cornelis Struik House, 80 McKenzie Street, Cape Town 8001, South Africa
3/2 Aquatic Drive, Frenchs Forest, NSW 2086, Australia

EDITOR: Jenny Barrett
DESIGNER: Odette Marais
PHOTOGRAPHER: Juan Espi
STYLIST: Elaine Levitte
ILLUSTRATOR: Lara Volpert
TEMPLATE ILLUSTRATOR: Darren McLean

Reproduction by Unifoto (Pty) Ltd, Cape Town
Printed by Times Offset (M) Sdn Bhd

ISBN 1 85368 541 0 (h/b)
ISBN 1 85368 908 4 (p/b)

ACKNOWLEDGMENTS
I owe thanks to many people who helped to make this book possible – firstly, thanks to Ian, my family and friends for their support, and to Zoe Henshaw and Lauren Morris for helping to make the projects; thank you to Linda de Villiers of Struik Publishers for her encouragement and faith in me, and also at Struik, Jenny Barrett and Odette Marais for all their hard work; to Juan Espi for many patient hours behind the camera, and to Dudley Fillies for assisting. Lara Volpert, thank you for the beautiful illustrations. A special note of thanks to the following shops for the generous loan of accessories for the photographs: Mystique, Collector's Corner, Outdoor Lifestyle, Block and Chisel, Clarewood Antiques and Interiors, Boardmans, Stuttafords, Biggie Best (Claremont), Peter Visser Interiors, The Yellow Door and The Fresh Flower Company. A big thank you to Belinda Wilkinson of Chinaworks for her lovely hand-painted plates that inspired the projects in the 'Bright for breakfast' chapter.
And last but not least, I must mention my dog and cats whose undemanding companionship means so much to me,
and Alessi whom I will miss forever.